Acknowledgement

This book is dedicated to every American family suffering through the hardships associated with losing their jobs in the name of "The Global Economy"; To every parent who can't offer their child or children the same opportunities our generation enjoyed; and finally, to the young people who will shoulder the burden of providing for those who allowed this to happen.

NAFTA

EMBRACING

CHANGE

In a few moments I will sign three agreements that will complete our negotiations with Mexico and Canada to create A North American Free Trade Agreement....

...NAFTA means jobs, American jobs, and good paying jobs. If I didn't believe that, I would not support the agreement.

...Ours is now an era in which Commerce is GLOBAL and in which money, management and technology are highly mobile.

...This debate over NAFTA is a debate over whether we will embrace CHANGE and create the jobs of tomorrow.

The North American Free Trade Agreement—President Bill Clinton's Speech To The Nation.

...I believe NAFTA will create 200,000 American jobs in the first five years. And I believe that is many more than will be lost, as inevitably some will be.

...I will sign side agreements to NAFTA that will make it harder than it is today for businesses to relocate solely because of very cheap wages or lax environmental rules. These side agreements will make a difference.

...In Mexico the working people...they'll have more disposable income to buy more American products, and there will be less illegal immigration. Mexicans will be able to support their families by staying home.

...ECONOMIC CHANGE, as I said before, has often been cruel to the middle class, but we have to make CHANGE our friends. NAFTA WILL HELP DO THAT.

...WE HAVE TO CREATE A NEW WORLD ECONO-MY...

WE WANT OUR JOBS BACK

Your Vote Cost
Us Our Jobs

Now Our Vote May
Cost You Your Job

Introduction

In January 1989 I accepted a management position with a transportation company looking to expand into Tennessee.

We moved into a vacant facility north of Jackson, Tennessee and began calling on potential customers in the area.

As we began making sales calls to introduce ourselves and our company to the various individuals who control shipping and receiving in our area, I started to develop working relationships and even friendships with many of them. I spent time with them every week either at their facility, having lunch, playing golf or just telephone conversations.

In 1993 President Bill Clinton was successful in pushing NAFTA through congress and signed it into law. It was not long before many of the manufacturers we were doing business with began moving portions of their operations out of the country.

Clinton followed the NAFTA agreement with two world trade agreements. The one he was most proud of was the agreement he signed with China. As a matter of fact, he considered that agreement to be the centerpiece of his entire presidency.

Gradually more and more of the manufacturers we were doing business with moved their entire operations out of the country; closed their doors completely; or, sold to competitors.

"FOR SALE" signs began appearing in front of vacant buildings all across our service area and the people I had come to know had to move on to find work in other places. Before long I was standing with my regional manager telling our people we were closing because we could not maintain the level of business required to keep our doors open.

This book is a tribute to all those families who lost their livelihoods, their homes, their friends, and their way of life. As we know, businesses are often measured in terms of the number of employees they have, but it is not just the employee who has his life devastated when a business closes, but the entire family.

President's Quotes

John F Kennedy-
-Our problems are man-made, therefore they may be solved by man. No problem of human destiny is beyond human beings.

John F. Kennedy-
-It is our task in our time and in our generation to hand down undiminished to those who come after us, as was handed down to us by those who went before, the natural wealth and beauty which is ours.

Ronald Reagan-
-The best minds are not in government. If any were, business would hire them away.

Ronald Reagan-
-The government's view of the economy could be summed up in a few short phrases: If it moves, tax it; If it keeps moving, regulated it; And, if it stops moving, subsidize it.

Ronald Reagan-
-Entrepreneurs and their small enterprises are responsible for almost all the economic growth in the United States.

Table of Contents

Chapter One

NAFTA

"We believe that if men have the talent to invent new machines that put men out of work, they have the talent to put those men back to work."   ---John F. Kennedy

President Bill Clinton signs NAFTA into law. Below, Barack Obama and Hillary Clinton debate the repeal of the jobs-killing agreement as part of the 2008 Democratic Party Presidential Primary.

ROSS PEROT AND VICE-PRESIDENT AL GORE DEBATE NAFTA

GORE: …

We believe NAFTA will create 200,000 American jobs
in the first two years and one million American jobs in
the first five years…

…We believe the side agreements will make a difference.

…NAFTA will make it harder to relocate solely because of
low wages or lax environmental rules...

…The Mexican people will have more disposable income
to buy more American products and they will be able
to support their families by staying home. That means less
illegal immigration...

PEROT: …Do you guys ever do anything but propaganda?...

…would you even know the truth if you saw it? I don' t believe
you would. You've been up here too long

…Here's how you get out of it (NAFTA). If the House of
Representatives lets this go through. The whole House
Of Representatives is running in 1994 and one-third of
the Senate. We've got a little song we sing "We'll
remember in November" when we step in that little booth.
If we have to, We The People, the owners of the country,
will clean this mess up in Washington…

"THE GIANT SUCKING SOUND"

Ross Perot was right. Bill Clinton, Hillary Clinton, Al Gore, and all the Republicans who voted with Clinton were completely wrong about the long term effects of NAFTA.

CHAPTER TWO

Clothing
And
Textiles

Lost jobs in the clothing and textile industry in West Tennessee

GARAN INCORPORATED
Dorsky Drive
Adamsville, TN.
Shirts   1986   employed   350

LEAPWOOD MFG COMPANY
Route 2
Adamsville, TN.
Men's and boys' sport shirts
1977   employed   85

TN. RIVER MFG
Highway 64, East
Adamsville, TN.
Shirts   1981   employed   91

ALAMO MILLS
344 South Mills Street
Alamo, TN
Ladies' lingerie
1987   employed   100

ANGELICA UNIFORM GROUP
Route 2
Alamo, TN
Uniforms and career apparel
1985   employed   90

WSW COMPANY
Atwood Plant/ 2nd Street
Atwood, TN
Pajamas and sportswear
1974   employed   200

HILL,MURRAY MFG COMPNAY
Route 3
Bethel Springs, TN
Ladies' blouses
1982   employed   32

MASTER SLACK CORPORATION
Highway 18, South
Bolivar, TN
Men's ad boy's pants
1963   employed   161

WSW MFG COMPANY
Alexander Street
Bradford, TN
Children's sleepwear
1980   employed   126

JAMES H. MOORE & SON GARMENT CO.
1009 N. Washington Avenue
Brownsville, TN
Ladies' and children's sportswear
1973   employed   100

HENRY I. SIEGEL COMPANY, Inc.
313 Rowland Mill Road
Bruceton, TN
Jeans   1940   employed   750

BASS MFG
Highway 70, West
Camden, TN.
Women's apparel   1976   employed   99

OSHKOSH B'GOSH, INCORPORATED
Industrial Road
Camden, TN
Children's half-elastic jeans
1986   employed   300

HENRY I. SIEGEL COMPANY
Industrial Road
Camden, TN
Sportswear   1977   employed   210

CADILLAC CURTAIN CORPORATION
Highway 51, North
Covington, TN
Curtains and drapes
1961   employed   90

JONES COMPANIES, INC.
Mill Road
Covington, TN.
Mop Yarn   1964   employed   40

RIVER HEIGHTS MFG. COMPANY
Highway 64
Crump, TN
Men's and boys' shirts
1977   employed   80

DECATURVILLE MFG. COMPANY, INC.
641 South
Decaturville, TN
Ladies' sportswear
1985   employed   125

DECATURVILLE SPORTSWEAR CO., INC.
Main Street
Decaturville, TN
Ladies' sportswear
1960   employed   500

DYERSBURG FABRICs, INC
East Phillips Street
Dyersburg, TN
Synthetics   1929   employed   931

HENRY I. SIEGEL COMPNAY, INC.
606 College Street
Gleason, TN
Ladies "Chic" jeans
1935   employed   205

C&P MFG. COMPANY
212 Front Street
Greenfield, TN
Garments and shirts
1984   employed   75

KELLWOOD COMPANY-
PLANT OUTERWEAR DIVISION
Greenfield, TN
Ladies' outwear
1947   employed   400

CHESTER COUNTY SPORTSWEAR
Highway 100 East
Henderson, TN.
Pants   1982   employed   390

HENDERSON LEISUREWEAR, INC.
122 South Franklin Street
Henderson, TN.
Ladies' robes   1981   employed   176

LEXINGTON APPAREL CORP
First Street
Lexington, TN.
Men's and boys slacks
1985   employed 168

PUBLIX SHIRT CORPORATION
230 Murray Lane
Men's and boys' shirts
1947   employed   400

IFC NONWOVENS, INC.
20 Phillips Road
Jackson, TN.
Fabricator/converter of nonwoven
Textiles for industry and health care
1976   employed   100

LEE COMPANY
Madison West Industrial Park
140 Whalley Drive
Laundering jeans
1987   employed   130

TENNESSEE TEXTILES, INC.
Bemis, TN.
Industrial twine, sheeting and woven
Industrial fabrics, knitting and
Weaving sales yarn
1900   employed   624

DECATURVILLE SPORTSWEAR COMPANY
LEXINGTON DIVISION
Natchez Trace Drive
Lexington, TN.
Women's sportswear
1977   employed   137

LEXINGTON APPAREL CORPORATION
First Street
Lexington, TN.
Men's and boys' slacks
1985   employed   168

MARTIN MFG COMPANY, INC.
Highway 22 East
Martin, TN.
Military shirts
1954   employed   475

CHARLES TODD INCORPORATED
Maury City, TN.
Uniform shirts, coats, jackets
And ladies' toppers
1976   employed   108

WEN-SU MANUFACTURING COMPANY
227 North Highland Drive
McKenzie, TN.
Sportswear   1985   employed   180

O'BRYAN BROTHES MFG COMPANY
McLemoresville, TN.
Men's Duckhead trousers and shorts
1985   employed 71

SEEGULL MFG COMPANY
Milan, TN.
Clothing stitching operation
Unknown date   employed   110

ALL-WEAR MFG COMPANY, INC.
Newbern, TN.
Girls' ladies' boys' and men's sportswear
1961   employed   375

OBION COMPANY
SALANT CORPORATION DIVISION
Troy Road
Obion, TN.
Sleepwear   1942   employed   176

PARIS FASHION, INC.
205 East Washington Street
Paris, TN.
Clothing   1982   employed   100

ROBINSON MFG COMPNAY
Hwy 412
Parsons, TN.
Gym shorts, athletic wear
1981   employed   170

ACTION APPAREL, INC.
Highway 57
Ramer, TN.
Sportswear   1979   employed   100

APPAREL NETWORK
395 Dillard Street
Ridgely, TN.
Ladies' ready-to-wear
1970   employed   100

ROLANE INDUSTRIES
Dillard Street
Ridgely, TN.
Jackets and coats
1960   employed   150

MASTER CASUAL WEAR
Ripley, TN.
Men's casual slacks
1966   employed   200

TODDRIPCO
North Industrial Park
Ripley, TN.
Men's work clothes and rental uniforms
1971   employed   170

KELLWOOD COMPANY
Rutherford, TN.
Coats and jackets
1941   employed   540

HIS SPORTSWEAR INCORPORATED
Campsite Road
Saltillo, TN.
Ladies" apparel
1957   employed   220

TENNESSEE RIVER MFG
Route 1
Sardis, TN.
Men's and boys' shirts
1987   employed   30

JETRICKS COMPANY, INC.
Highway 45, North
Selmer, TN.
Shirts   1972   employed   150

SOMERVILLE MILLS
Highway 59, North
Somerville, TN.
Ladies' panties
1983   employed   325

HENRY I. SIEGEL, MFG COMPANY
South Fulton, TN.
Sportswear   1959   employed   489

U.S. APPAREL INCORPORATED
Route 1
Stantonville, TN.
Sports clothes   1977   employed   90

HENRY I. SIEGEL COMPANY, INC.
Main Street
Trezevant, TN.
Jeans   1947   employed   205

TROY MFG COMPANY
Polk Road
Troy, TN.
Boy's pants, children's playclothes
1968   employed   310

The Ten Fastest Dying U.S. Industries

ABC News aired a report on April 5, 2011 on their Money segment concerning ten United States Industries that are actually dead already or heading that way FAST.

The report suggested that these industries strap on a "Do Not Resuscitate" sign and pull the shades down.

Number four on their list was the Textile Industry and number six was the Apparel Industry.

The ABC News report was based on a report by the market research company, IBIS World. IBIS World boasts being "the largest provider of industry information in the United States."

To add insult to injury for all of us who lost our livelihoods when these industries left the U.S. in search of cheap labor, the program was presented by George Stephanopoulos, the White House spokesman for Bill Clinton who pushed NAFTA and other trade agreements through Congress.

These agreements opened the door for these and other industries to move their operations to Mexico and China.

U.S. Textile Makers are seeking tariffs against Chinese imports because:

- Chinese fabrics are entering the U.S. duty free through foreign trade zone operations in North Carolina and Mississippi.

- Chinese goods have flooded the market at record rates and at uncompetitive prices.

- Chinese companies grabbed market share at the expense of the American textile manufacturers.

- The petition claims that the Chinese government subsidizes the textile producers, and keeps the Chinese currency under valued which makes products cheaper in U.S. dollars.

- One manufacturing executive quoted in the report said that if he had **FREE LABOR**, his fabric would sell for 20% less, but **Chinese-goods would still be 50% cheaper.**

Dyersburg Fabrics, Dyersburg, Tennessee

Founded 1929   Employed 931

Kellwood Company   Rutherford, Tennessee

Established 1941   Employed 600

Henry I. Siegel Company   Bruceton, Tennessee

Established 1940   22   Employed 750

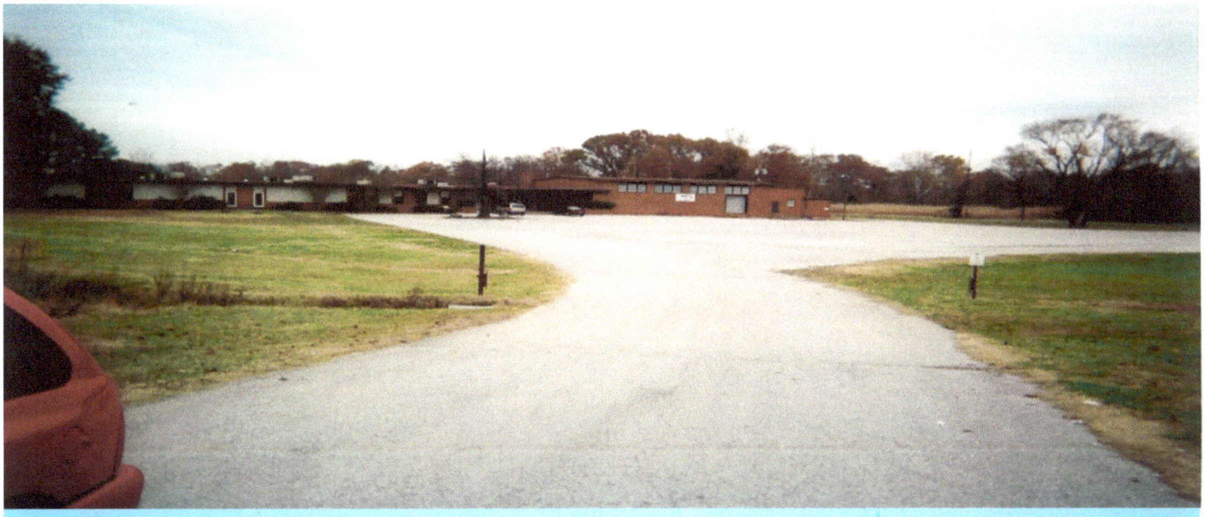

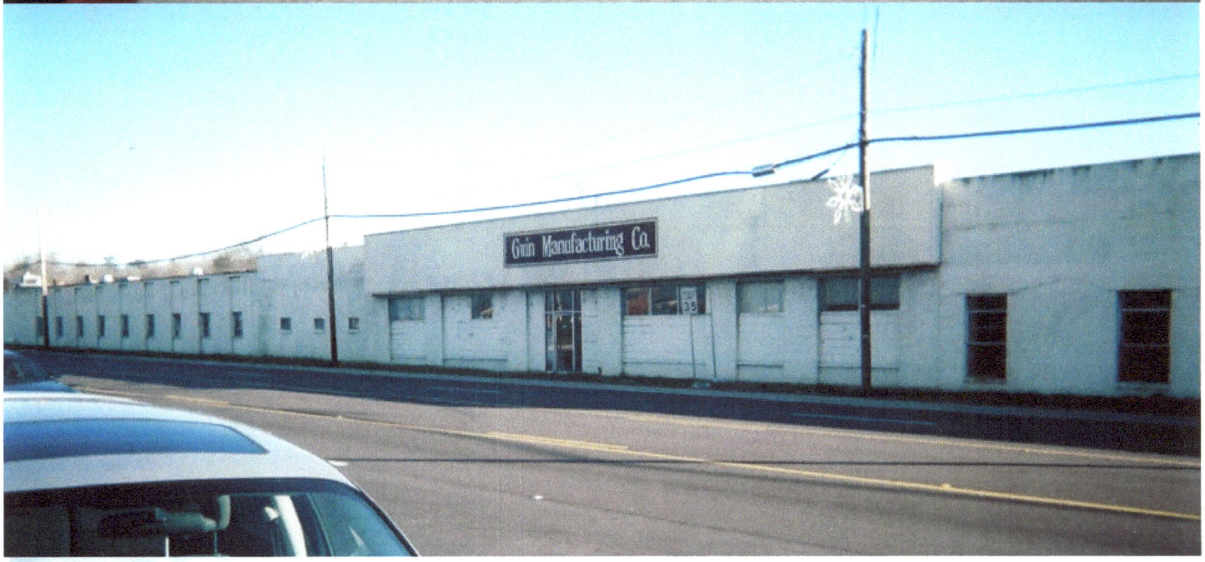

Gwin Manufacturing Co.
35

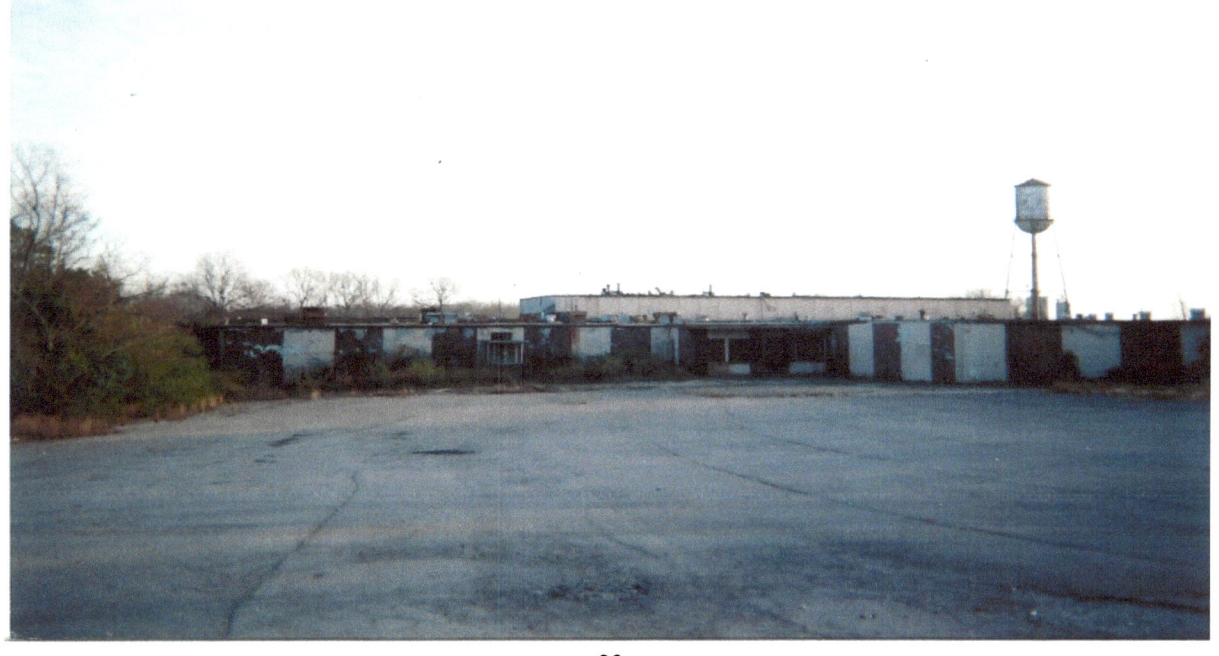

CHAPTER THREE

THE AUTOMOTIVE INDUSTRY

"In today's GLOBAL ECONOMY, there's not an easy way to determine just how AMERICAN a car is."

Patrick Olse
Cars.com Editor In Chief

Toyota Camry "Most American Car"

Cars.Com announced today that the Toyota Camry once again took top spot in the site's annual American Made Index.

This is the third consecutive year the Camry has held this position, despite many newcomers to the list including the Ford Explorer, the Chevrolet Traverse and the GMC Acadia. The Camry, which is assembled in Georgetown, Kentucky and Lafayette, Indiana is followed by the Honda Accord and the Chevy Malibu, which rank number two and number three respectively.

Cars.Com's annual American Made Index ranks the most American made vehicles based on the percentage of their parts that are made domestically, where they are assembled and how many are sold to U.S. buyers.

"In today's Global Economy, there's not an easy way to determine just how American a car is," said Patrick Olsen, Cars.Com's Editor-in-Chief.

"Most cars built in the United States for example, are assembled somewhere else. Additionally, many U.S. automakers assemble vehicles in Canada and Mexico, while foreign automakers have opened plants on U.S. soil."

"Our index is another resource that buyers can use to help guide their purchase decisions," said Olsen.

Domestic parts content is based on data that appears alongside the window sticker of new cars as a result of the American Automotive Labeling Act, passed in 1994. The act mandates that virtually every new car display the percentage, by cost, of its parts that originate in the United States and Canada. Only those vehicles with a domestic parts content rating of 75% or higher are eligible for the American Made Index.

Cars.Com's Most American Made Index For 2011

Rank	Make/Model	U.S. Assy Location	Rank in 2010
1	Toyota Camry	Georgetown, Ky.	1
2	Honda Accord	Marysville, Ohio	2
3	Chevy Malibu	Kansas City, Ks.	5
4	Ford Explorer	Chicago, Illinois	-
5	Honda Odyssey	Lincoln, Alabama	6
6	Toyota Sienna	Princeton, Indiana	10
7	Jeep Wrangler	Toledo, Ohio	9
8	Chevy Traverse	Lansing, Mi.	-
9	Toyota Tundra	San Antonio, Texas	8
10	GMC Acadia	Lansing, Michigan	-

General Motors lead the list of the big three "domestic automakers" with three models. However, their Silverado series pickup line failed to make the list again this year coming in with only 61% of its parts being "domestic parts." (Made in the United States or Canada).

Here is the list of General Motors parts suppliers from Wikipedia.org/wiki/list-of-GM factories website:

List of General Motors factories

From Wikipedia, the free encyclopedia
 (Redirected from List of GM factories)

This is a **list of General Motors factories** currently or previously used to produce automobiles and automobile components.[1] The factories are occasionally idled for re-tooling.

Contents

- 1 Current GM factories
- 2 Closed or sold GM factories
- 3 See also
- 4 Notes

Current GM factories

VIN	Name	City/State	Country	Products	Opened	Idled	Comments
	6th of October City	6th of October City	Egypt	Astra Corsa N-Series Rodeo TF-Series Vectra	1985		
R	Arlington Assembly	Arlington, Texas	USA	Escalade Suburban Tahoe Yukon Yukon XL	1953		Past models: GM A platform (RWD), GM G platform, and GM B platform
	Baltimore Transmission	Baltimore, Maryland	USA	1000 Series transmissions: Silverado, Sierra Hybrid 2-mode transmissions: Tahoe, Escalade, Silverado, Sierra	2000		Originally part of Allison Transmission. Became a GM Powertrain facility in 2004.
	Barcelona	Barcelona	Spain	Opel/Vauxhall Vivaro Renault Trafic Nissan Primastar			Nissan plant
	Batilly	Batilly	France	Opel/Vauxhall Movano Renault Master/Mascott Nissan Interstar			Renault-SOVAB plant
	Bay City Powertrain	Bay City, Michigan	USA	Engine components	1916		
	Bedford Powertrain	Bedford, Indiana	USA	Transmission casings	1942		
	Bochum	Bochum	Germany	Opel/Vauxhall Zafira	1962		Adam Opel AG Opel plant
	Bogotá	Bogotá	Colombia	Alto, Bus, Corsa, Esteem, Jimny, Kodiak, LUV, D-MAX, N-Series, Sprint (not the same one as sold in the US and Canada), Super Carry, Swift, Aveo, Optra, Spark, Astra, Zafira, Wagon R+, Vitara			
5	Bowling Green Assembly Plant	Bowling Green, Kentucky	USA	Corvette	1981		Past models: XLR
6	CAMI Automotive	Ingersoll, Ontario	Canada	Chevrolet Equinox GMC Terrain	1988		Past models:Tracker, Sidekick, Asuna/Pontiac Sunrunner (Canada only), Suzuki Vitara, Chevrolet/Geo Metro, Pontiac Firefly (Canada only), Suzuki Swift, Suzuki XL-7, Pontiac Torrent.
	Changwon	Gyeongsang	South Korea	Damas Labo Matiz			

B	Daewoo Incheon Motor Company	Bupyung, Incheon	South Korea	Kalos Aveo Magnus		Suzuki Verona
	Dandenong	Victoria	Australia	Holden	1956	Manufacturing ceased in 1988, minor assembly until 1996, now parts distribution warehouse
	Defiance Foundry	Defiance, Ohio	USA	Aluminum/iron engine blocks	1948	
	Delco Moraine NDH	Moraine, Ohio (Wisconsin Blvd.)	USA	Engine Bearings/Master Cylinders/Brake Pads/Brake Calipers/ABS Assemblies		
	Delco Moraine NDH	Dayton, Ohio (Needmore Rd.)	USA	Master Cylinders/Brake Pads/Brake Calipers/ABS Assemblies		
	Delco Moraine NDH	Sandusky, Ohio	USA	Wheel Bearings & Wheel Bearing Assemblies		
	Delco Moraine NDH	Fredericksburg, Virginia	USA	components		
	Delco Products	Kettering, Ohio	USA	Shock Absorbers, Struts, Impact Absorbers, Electric Motors, Windshield Wiper Assemblies		Transferred to Delphi Automotive Systems in 1999. Sold to Tenneco Corporation in 2008
	Delco Remy	Anderson, Indiana	USA	Starters, Generators, HEI Ignition, DIS Ignition, Switches	2006	Transferred to Delphi Automotive Systems in 1999
	Delco Remy	Muncie, Indiana	USA	Batteries		Transferred to Delphi Automotive Systems in 1999.
U	Detroit/Hamtramck Assembly	Hamtramck, Michigan & Detroit, Michigan	USA	DTS Lucerne Volt	1985	aka "Poletown" Past models: Deville, Seville
	Eisenach	Eisenach	Germany	Opel/Vauxhall Corsa	1990	Adam Opel AG Opel plant
L	Elizabeth	Elizabeth, South Australia	Australia	Adventra Berlina Calais Caprice Commodore Crewman Crewman Cross 8 Cruze Monaro (Pontiac GTO) Pontiac G8 One Tonner Statesman/Caprice Ute Vectra	1960	Holden Holden Motor Company
	Ellesmere Port	Ellesmere Port	United Kingdom	Opel/Vauxhall Astra	1962	Vauxhall Motors plant
F	Fairfax II	Fairfax, Kansas	USA	Chevrolet Malibu Buick LaCrosse	1987	Past models: Oldsmobile Cutlass Supreme (1995 & 1996), Pontiac Grand Prix (1988–2003), Saturn Aura, Chevrolet Equinox.
	Flint Engine South	Flint, Michigan	USA	3.6 High Feature engine, 1.4 (Cruze, Volt generator)	2000	Past engines: Atlas I6
	Flint East	Flint, Michigan	USA	components		Now part of Delphi Corporation, returned to GM in 2009
	Flint Metal Center	Flint, Michigan	USA		1954	Metal fabricating
	Flint Tool & Die	Flint, Michigan	USA		1967	Metal fabricating
F	Flint Truck Assembly	Flint, Michigan	USA	Silverado/Sierra (light and heavy duty)	1947	Past models: Kodiak/Topkick, Corvair Forward Control
Z	Fort Wayne Assembly	Roanoke, Indiana	USA	Silverado/Sierra	1986	

7	Fujisawa	Fujisawa, Kanagawa	Japan	Chevrolet LUV		Isuzu manufacturing facility
	Gliwice	Gliwice	Poland	Opel/Vauxhall Astra Opel/Vauxhall Astra Classic	1998	Adam Opel AG Opel plant
	GM Daewoo Vietnam Auto & Technology	Hanoi	Vietnam	Lanos Magnus Nubira		
	GMM Luton Vehicles[2]	Luton	United Kingdom	Opel/Vauxhall Vivaro Renault Trafic Nissan Primastar	1905	Vauxhall Motors plant
	Grand Blanc Metal Center	Grand Blanc, Michigan	USA		1942	Metal casting
	Gravatai Automotive Industrial Complex	Gravatai, Rio Grande do Sul	Brazil	Chevrolet Celta	2000	[1] (http://www.autointell.com /nao_companies/general_motors /gm-manufacturing/blue-macaw-01.htm) [2] (http://www.reuters.com /article/idUSN1533675720090715)
	Guide Headlamp Division	Anderson, Indiana	USA	Headlamp, Taillamp assemblies		
	Gunsan	Jeolla	South Korea	Lacetti Rezzo		
	Halol	Halol,Gujrat	India	Chevrolet Cruze Chevrolet Aveo		Past models: Opel Corsa Opel Astra
	Indianapolis Metal Center	Indianapolis, Indiana	USA		1930	Metal fabricating Scheduled to close 12/2011
	Inland Fisher Guide Plant (Euclid, Ohio)	Euclid, Ohio	USA	Seat Covers & Backs		
	Inland Fisher Guide Plant (Vandalia, Ohio)	Vandalia, Ohio	USA	Door Panel Assemblies Seat Pads Instrument Panels	1941	Originally a GM Aeroproducts facility, absorbed by Inland division in 1955, spun off to Inland Fisher Guide division in 1991, became part of Delphi in 1996 and transferred to Delphi Thermal Division in 2007.
	Inland Fisher Guide Plant (Tecumseh, Michigan)	Tecumseh, Michigan	USA	Seat Pads & Backs		
	Inland Fisher Guide Plant (Livonia, Michigan)	Livonia, Michigan	USA	Seat Cushions, Seat Pads, Seat Backs, Door Panel Trim]]	1954	
4	Iwata	Iwata, Shizuoka	Japan			
3	Kawasaki	Kawasaki, Kanagawa	Japan			
K	Kosai Assembly	Kosai, Shizuoka	Japan			
	Lansing Service Parts Operation	Delta Township, Michigan	USA		1959	SPO
J	Lansing Delta Township Assembly	Delta Township, Michigan	USA	Chevrolet Traverse GMC Acadia Buick Enclave	2006	
	Lansing Regional Stamping	Delta Township, Michigan	USA		2003	LRS
0	Lansing Grand River Assembly	Lansing, Michigan	USA	CTS STS	2001	
5	London	London, Ontario	Canada			
7	Lordstown Assembly	Lordstown, Ohio	USA	Cruze	1966	Past models: Cobalt/G5, Cavalier/Sunbird/Sunfire
7	Magyar Suzuki Corporation	Esztergom	Hungary	Opel/Vauxhall Agila Suzuki Splash Suzuki Swift Suzuki SX4 Fiat Sedici	1991	Suzuki plant
	Marion Metal Center	Marion, Indiana	USA		1956	Metal fabricating

	Norwich	Norwich	United Kingdom	Speedster VX220		
	General Motors del Ecuador - Omnibus BB	Quito	Ecuador	Bus D-Max 2011 Tahoe 2011 Hybrid Captiva 2010 Vitara 2011 Aveo GT 2011 Spark GT 2011 Optra 2011 Limited Vitara		
4	Orion Assembly	Orion Township, Michigan	USA		1983	Idled in 2009. Will reopen in 2011 to produce the Chevrolet Sonic and Buick Verano. Past models: Malibu, G6
1	Oshawa Car Assembly	Oshawa, Ontario	Canada	Impala Camaro Equinox	1953	Past models: LaCrosse/Allure, Corvair Cars
	Oshawa Metal	Oshawa, Ontario	Canada			
	Parma Metal Center	Parma, Ohio	USA		1948	Metal fabricating
	Pontiac Metal Center	Pontiac, Michigan	USA		1929	Metal fabricating
	Port Melbourne (Fishermans Bend)	Victoria	Australia	Holden	1936	Headquarters of GM Holden Ltd Holden Engine Company
S	Ramos Arizpe	Ramos Arizpe	Mexico	Chevrolet C2 Chevrolet HHR Cadillac SRX	1981	
	Rayong	Rayong	Thailand	Colorado Cruze Optra Aveo Captiva	1999	Past Models: Zafira, Alfa Romeo 156 [3] (http://www.just-auto.com /article.aspx?id=79416)
	Romulus Engine	Romulus, Michigan	USA	4.3L V6 Gen IV V8	1976	Engines
	Romulus Transmission	Romulus, Michigan	USA		1995	Transmissions
	Rosario	Rosario	Argentina	Corsa Chevrolet Corsa Combo Agile	1997	Past Models: Grand Blazer, Silverado, Chevrolet Corsa II and Grand Vitara
R	Rüsselsheim	Rüsselsheim	Germany	Opel/Vauxhall Insignia	1898	Adam Opel AG Opel plant
	Saginaw Metal Casting Operations	Saginaw, Michigan	USA		1919	Metal casting for powertrains. Engine Blocks. Crankshafts
	Saginaw Transmission	Saginaw, Michigan	USA	Manual Transmissions, Brakes		Originally made the "Saginaw" 3 and 4-Speed manual transmissions. The plant currently produces brake components. It was spun off as part of Delphi in 1999. The plant is currently owned by TRW Automotive.
	San Luis Potosí Assembly	San Luis Potosí	Mexico	Chevrolet Aveo Pontiac G3 Pontiac Wave	2008	
	São Caetano do Sul	São Caetano do Sul, São Paulo	Brazil	Astra Corsa Classic Cruze Vectra	1930	
	São José dos Campos	São José dos Campos, São Paulo	Brazil	Blazer Meriva Montana Corsa C S-10 Zafira		

VIN	Name	City/State	Country	Products	Opened	Comments
8	Shreveport Operations	Shreveport, Louisiana	USA	Colorado Canyon	1981	Past models: GMT325 and 330 pickup trucks (S and T-series), H3
G	Silao Assembly	Silao	Mexico	Escalade ESV Escalade EXT Avalanche Suburban Yukon XL	1994	
Z/S	Spring Hill Manufacturing	Spring Hill, Tennessee	USA	Ecotec 2.0 Turbo Ecotec 2.4 Stamping Components (Traverse)	1990	Vue production moved to Mexico for 2008 model year Assembly idled in 2009. Past models: Ion, Vue, S-Series, Traverse
	St. Catharines Engine	St. Catharines, Ontario	Canada		1954	
3	St. Eustache	Saint-Eustache, Quebec	Canada			
	Struandale	Port Elizabeth	South Africa	Astra Corsa F-Series N-Series TF-Series H3		
T	Tarrytown Truck Assembly	Tarrytown, New York	USA			Truck and Bus. Also home to these past models: Century Bonneville Trans Sport van
9	Tillonsburg Assembly	Tillsonburg, Ontario	Canada			
	GM-AvtoVAZ	Tolyatti	Russia	Niva Viva	2002	
	Toledo Transmission	Toledo, Ohio	USA	6L80 RWD 6-speed Global FWD 6-speed	1956	Future product: GF6 6T30/6T45/BAS Hybrid
	Tonawanda Engine	Tonawanda, New York	USA	Ecotec 2.2 Ecotec 2.4 Vortec 2.9 I4 Vortec 3.7 I5	1937	Past engines: Corvair (all)
	Valencia	Valencia	Venezuela	Astra Corsa Impala Kodiak TrailBlazer GMT800 Grand Vitara Wagon R		
	Warren Transmission	Warren, Michigan	USA	6T70, 6T75	1941	Past transmissions: Hydramatic
1	Wentzville Assembly	Wentzville, Missouri	USA	Express Savana	1983	Past models: Buick Electra/Park Avenue, Oldsmobile 98, Pontiac Bonneville, (1992-93)
	Willow Run Transmission	Ypsilanti, Michigan	USA	4L80-E transmission 4T80-E transmission	1953	
	Wixom Performance Build Center	Wixom, Michigan	USA	6.2L V8 LS3 7.0L V8 LS7 6.2L V8 LS9	2004	;
	Zaragoza	Figueruelas	Spain	Opel/Vauxhall Corsa Opel/Vauxhall Meriva	1982	Adam Opel AG Opel plant

Closed or sold GM factories

VIN	Name	City/State	Country	Products	Opened	Idled	Comments

		Location	Country	Products	Opened	Closed	Notes
	AC Rochester	Wichita Falls, Texas	USA	AC Air Filters	1972	2008	Transferred to Delphi Automotive Systems in 1999. Closed by Delphi in 2008
	AC Rochester	Sioux City, Iowa	USA	Throttle Body Fuel Injection Systems	1981	1993	Formerly a Zenith Radio Factory[3]
	Acacia Ridge	Acacia Ridge, Queensland	Australia	Holden	1967	1985	
	Allison Transmission	Indianapolis, Indiana	USA	Allison transmissions	1915		Sold in 2007 to private equity firm
	Antwerp	Antwerp	Belgium	Opel/Vauxhall /Saturn Astra Opel/Vauxhall Astra TwinTop	1924	2011	
	Arica	Arica	Chile	LUV D-Max	1974	2008	Past models: Canadian C-10 and C-30, Brazilian Chevette, Japanese Aska and LUV
	Azambuja	Azambuja	Portugal	Opel/Vauxhall Combo	1959	2006	
B	Baltimore Assembly	Baltimore, Maryland	USA	Astro Safari	1935	2005	Truck and Bus
H	Buick City	Flint, Michigan	USA		1904	1999	Past models: Bonneville, LeSabre
9	Detroit Assembly	Detroit, Michigan	USA	Cadillacs	1921	1987	Redeveloped in to Clark Street Technology Park in 1997
C	Diesel Division	London, Ontario	Canada	New Look (1961–1974) locomotives	1950		Transit bus production moved to Saint-Eustache factory in 1974. Sold in 2005, renamed Electro-Motive Diesel.
M	Diesel Division Saint-Eustache	Saint-Eustache, Quebec	Canada	New Look Classic	1974		Manufactures transit buses. Sold to Motor Coach Industries, along with the designs for the bus models this factory produced, in 1987; currently owned by Nova Bus.
D	Doraville Assembly	Doraville, Georgia	USA	Terraza Uplander SV6 Relay	1947	2008	Past models: Venture, Silhouette
X	Fairfax Assembly	Fairfax, Kansas	USA		1947	1987	Production moved to new building on adjacent site
	Flint North Components	Flint, Michigan	USA	3800		2010	
G	Framingham Assembly	Framingham, Massachusetts	USA	A-bodies	1947	1989	
	GMPT Fredericksburg	Fredericksburg, Virginia	USA	Torque converter clutches for automatic transmissions	1979	2010	
Z	Fremont Assembly	Fremont, California	USA	Vibe Prizm (1990-2002) Nova (1985-88) Toyota vehicles	1960 1984	1982	1960-1982 as GM factory. From 1984 as New United Motor Manufacturing Inc. (NUMMI) (http://www.nummi.com) , which assembled GM and Toyota vehicles. Sold 7/2009.
	Grand Rapids Metal Center	Grand Rapids, Michigan	USA		1936	2009	Metal fabricating
7	Graz	Graz	Austria	Saab 9-3 Convertible			Magna Steyr plant
	Inland Plant	Dayton & Vandalia, Ohio	USA	Engine Mounts Transmission Mounts Strut Mounts Steering Wheels Liteflex Springs Brake Linings Brake Hose	1921	2008	Factory was started as the Dayton Wright Brothers Aeroplane Company in 1912, Bought as the Inland Corporation by GM in 1923. Transferred to Delphi Automotive Systems in 1999.

	Plant	Location	Country	Products	Opened	Closed	Notes
	Inland Fisher Guide Plant (New Jersey)	Ewing Township, New Jersey	USA	Brake Pads Ball Joints Ice Cube Trays door handles seat adjusters body moldings. Plant was known as the Turnstedt Plant	1938	1998	brief article about the plant's closing and displaced workers, 1993 Plant closing date delayed until Summer of 1998 : [4] (http://query.nytimes.com /gst/fullpage.html?res=9E0CEEDB1E3EF937A35751C1A964958260) Ternstedt Division and Photo http://wiki.gmnext.com/wiki/index.php /Ternstedt_Division
	Inland Fisher Guide Plant (Columbus, Ohio)	Columbus, Ohio	USA	Door Panel Assemblies & Small Components	1946	2007	Originally opened as a plant for the Ternstedt Division of General Motors; Transferred to Delphi Automotive Systems in 1999
J	Janesville Assembly	Janesville, Wisconsin	USA	Suburban Tahoe Tiltmaster Forward Yukon Yukon XL	1919	2008	Oldest GM assembly plant; largest under one roof in the U.S.; Idled Dec 23, 2008.
A	Lakewood Assembly	Lakewood, Georgia	USA		1927	1990	Production ended with Chevrolet Caprice Classic, Buick Estate Wagon, and Oldsmobile Custom Cruiser
	Lansing Engine	Delta Township, Michigan	USA		1981	2001	Built to produce experimental diesel engine; part of Ryder Logistics since 2005
	Lansing Car Assembly - Body	Lansing, Michigan	USA		1920	2005	Body
M	Lansing Car Assembly - Chassis	Lansing, Michigan	USA		1902	2005	M
B	Lansing Craft Centre	Lansing, Michigan	USA	SSR	1987	2006	Past models: Reatta, EV1
	Lansing Metal Center	Lansing, Michigan	USA		1952	2006	Metal fabricating
K	Leeds Assembly	Kansas City, Missouri	USA			1988	Buick Skyhawk, Oldsmobile Firenza, Chevrolet Cavalier, Chevrolet El Camino
E	Linden Assembly	Linden, New Jersey	USA			2005	Chevrolet Blazer, GMC Jimmy, Buick Riviera, Oldsmobile Toronado, Cadillac Eldorado
	Livonia Engine	Livonia, Michigan	USA	Premium V engine	1971	2010	
	Mansfield Metal Center	Mansfield, Ohio	USA		1955	2010	Metal fabricating
	Massena Castings Plant	Massena, New York	USA		1959	2009	Cylinder heads, Engine Blocks Closed May 1, 2009
2	Moraine Assembly	Moraine, Ohio	USA	S-10 S-15 Rainier TrailBlazer Envoy Ascender 9-7X	1951	2008	Closed on December 23, 2008. Formerly site of truck and bus production. Began in 1951 as the Frigidaire Division of General Motors Corporation producing household appliances.
N	Norwood Assembly	Norwood, Ohio	USA	Bel Air Camaro Firebird	1923	1987	
6	Oklahoma City Assembly	Oklahoma City, Oklahoma	USA	TrailBlazer EXT Envoy XL Ascender	1979	2006	Previously produced front wheel drive X platform and N platform vehicles. Idled February 20, 2006.
	Oshawa Truck Assembly	Oshawa, Ontario	Canada	Silverado Sierra	1965	2009	
	Pagewood	Pagewood, New South Wales	Australia	Holden	1939	1981	

	Plant	Location	Country	Products	Opened	Closed	Notes
	Petone	Petone	New Zealand		1926	1984	
	Pittsburgh Metal	Pittsburgh, Pennsylvania	USA		1949	2007	Metal fabricating
P	Pontiac Assembly	Pontiac, Michigan	USA	Fiero G-bodies	1927	1988	
V	Pontiac Assembly Center	Pontiac, Michigan	USA	Silverado/Sierra	1972	2009	Formerly part of the Truck and Bus group
	Saginaw Malleable Iron	Saginaw, Michigan	USA		1919	2007	Iron castings. HQ of Central Foundry Division.
	Saginaw Steering Gear - Plant 2	Saginaw, Michigan	USA	Steering Gears, pump hoses	1941	2001	Affectionately known as "The Gun Plant", it was built in 1941 when the division was contracted to build M1919 machine guns, and M1-Carbines for World War II. After the war, normal steering gear production continued until it's closure in 2001. It has been demolished
	Saginaw Division	Saginaw, Michigan	USA	Complete Hydraulic and Electric Power Steering Systems, Halfshafts, Intermediate Drive Shafts	1957	2010	Former Saginaw Steering Division of GM. The sprawling Five-Plant complex, division Headquarters and large engineering center, were spun off with Delphi in 1999. GM re-purchased the Steering division from bankrupt Delphi in 2009, and then sold the division to Pacific Century Motors in 2010. The former GM Division now operates as "Nexteer Automotive", an independent company headquartered at the Saginaw site.
2	Sainte-Thérèse Assembly	Sainte-Thérèse, Quebec	Canada		1966	2002	Past models: Firebird, Camaro
4	Scarborough Van Assembly	Scarborough, Ontario	Canada	G-series vans GMC Vandura Chevy Sportvan GMC Handi-Van	1963	1993	Operations moved to Flint Truck Assembly
C	South Gate Assembly	South Gate, California	USA		1936	1982	First GM plant to build multi-carline body/chassis (Buick/Olds /Pontiac)serially. Other models: Tanks (WWII); Unibody BOP "Y" series Special, F85, Tempest added to B&C mix 1961-63; replaced by Chevrolet B for 64; Vega; Monza; Deville; Cavalier and Cimarron
S	St. Louis Truck Assembly	St. Louis, Missouri	USA			1987	Truck and Bus, Corvair Forward Control
M	Toluca Assembly	Toluca	Mexico	Medium Duty	1994	2008	
	Trentham	Trentham	New Zealand		1967	1990	
3	Trollhättan Assembly	Trollhättan	Sweden	Saab 9-3 Saab 9-5	1947		Saab Automobile sold to Spyker Cars in February, 2010.
L	Van Nuys Assembly	Van Nuys, California	USA	Camaro Firebird	1947	1992	Past models: Chevrolet Monte Carlo, Corvair, Pontiac GTO
W	Willow Run Assembly	Ypsilanti Twp, Michigan	USA		1959	1992	Past models: Corvair, Nova, Caprice, Custom Cruiser
Y	Wilmington Assembly	Wilmington, Delaware	USA	Solstice Sky Opel GT Daewoo GX2	1947	2009	Past models: Corsica, Beretta, Malibu, L-Series, Caprice/Impala
	Windsor Transmission	Windsor, Ontario	Canada	4T40/45E transmission	1920	2010	Previous 1920 -1928 axles and parts 1928 - 1963 engines
	Woodville	Woodville, South Australia	Australia	Holden	1923	1990	

See also

- List of former automotive manufacturing facilities
- List of Ford factories
- List of Chrysler factories

List of Ford factories

From Wikipedia, the free encyclopedia

The following is a list of current and former facilities of Ford Motor Company for manufacturing automobiles and other components. Per regulations, the factory is encoded into each vehicle's VIN as character 11 for North American models, and character 8 for European models.

For a listing of Ford's proving grounds and test facilities see Ford Proving Grounds.

Contents

- 1 Current Production Facilities
- 2 Former Production Facilities
- 3 See also
- 4 References

Current Production Facilities

VIN Code (NA/EU) ▶◀	Name ▶◀	City/State ▶◀	Country ▶◀	Status ▶◀	Employees ▶◀	Products	Comments
5 (NA)	AutoAlliance International	Flat Rock, Michigan	USA	Open	2,621	Ford Mustang Mazda 6	Built at site of closed Ford Michigan Casting Center
	AutoAlliance Thailand	Pleukdang	Thailand	Open	3,618	Ford Fiësta Ford Ranger Ford Everest Mazda 2 Mazda BT-50	
	Automobile Craiova	Craiova	Romania	Open		Ford Transit Connect Ford B-MAX (2010)	
P (EU)	Azambuja Assembly	Azambuja	Portugal			Ford Fiesta Ford Focus Ford Mondeo	
	Bahia Plant	Camaçari, Bahia	Brazil			Ford Fiesta Ford Fiesta Sedan Ford EcoSport	Plant opened in 2001 Scheduled to begin production for US market in 2009
V (NA)	Blue Diamond Truck	Escobedo General, Nuevo Leon	Mexico			Ford F-650 Ford F-750 Ford LCF	Commercial truck joint venture with Navistar
	Bordeaux Transaxle	Blanquefort	France	Open	947	Ford IB transmission	
	Bridgend Engine	Bridgend	Wales	Open	2,013	Ford Zetec engine Jaguar AJ-V8	

						engine	
JG JL (AU)	Broadmeadows Assembly	Campbellfield, Victoria	Australia	Open	2,088	Ford Falcon Ford Falcon Ute Ford Territory	
	Buffalo Stamping	Buffalo, New York	USA	Open	823	Quarter Panels, Body Sides, Rear Floor Pan, Rear Doors, Roofs, front doors, hoods	
J (EU)	Valencia Assembly	Valencia	Venezuela	Open			
	Changan Ford Mazda Engine Co.	Nanjing	China		700	BZ series engine	Joint Venture: Chongqing Changan Automobile Co., Ltd. (50%). Ford Motor Company (25%), Mazda Motor Company (25%)
G (NA)	Chicago Assembly	Chicago, Illinois	USA	Open	2,584	Ford Taurus Lincoln MKS Ford Explorer (Late 2010)	
	Chicago Stamping	Chicago Heights, Illinois	USA	Open	781		
	Chihuahua Engine	Chihuahua, Chihuahua	Mexico	Open	690	Duratec I4 4,4L and 6,7L V8 Diesel	Zetec engine (Discontinued)
	Cleveland Casting	Brook Park, Ohio	USA	To close (2010)	1,067	Engine blocks, crankshafts	
	Cleveland Engine #1	Brook Park, Ohio	USA	Reopened (2004)		Duratec 30 Duratec 35	Idled from May 2007 to May 2008
	Cleveland Engine #2	Brook Park, Ohio	USA	Open	813	Duratec 25 Duratec 30 RFF and DAMB	
A (EU)	Cologne Body & Assembly	Cologne	Germany	Open	4,141	Ford Fiesta Ford Fusion	
	Cologne Engine	Cologne	Germany	Open	1,008	Cologne V6	
	Cologne Forge and Die Cast	Cologne	Germany			parts	
	Cologne Tool and Die	Cologne	Germany	Open	1,144	equipment	
	Cologne Transmission	Cologne	Germany	Open	1,590	Ford MTX transmission Ford VXT transmission	

	Croydon Stamping	Croydon	England			parts
M (NA)	Cuautitlán Assembly	Cuautitlán-Izcalli	Mexico			Ford Fiesta
	Dagenham Engine	Dagenham	England	Open	2,047	Ford Duratorq engine Ford Duratec 20 Ford Duratec 23
	Dagenham Stamping	Dagenham	England	Open	1,084	
	Dagenham Tool & Die	Dagenham	England			equipment
	Dearborn Engine	Dearborn, Michigan	USA	Open	911	Ford Duratec 20 Ford Duratec 23 River Rouge Plant
	Dearborn Stamping	Dearborn, Michigan	USA	Open	588	Frames, Truck Axles, Suspension Parts, Tire and Wheel
F (NA)	Dearborn Truck	Dearborn, Michigan	USA			Ford F-150
	Ford Renaissance Global Logistics	Detroit, Michigan	USA			
	Essex Engine	Windsor, Ontario	Canada	Reopened (2009)		Ford Triton engine Ford Essex V6 engine Idled in November 2007, reopened February 2009
	Ford India, Ltd.	Tamil Nadu	India	Open	2,100	Ford Endeavour Ford Fiesta Ford Figo
	Ford India, Ltd.	Gujarat	India	To Open (2014)		
	Ford Lio Ho Assembly	Chung Li	Taiwan	Open	1,732	Ford Econovan Ford Fiesta Ford Mondeo Ford Pronto Ford Tierra Mazda 323 Mazda Bongo
	Ford Lio Ho Engine	Chung Li	Taiwan	Open	1,732	Ford Zetec engine
	Ford Malaysia Sdn. Bhd	Selangor	Malaysia	Open	705	Ford Laser Ford Telstar Ford Ranger Ford Econovan Ford Transit Ford Trader BMW Land Rover Discovery

Ford Motor Company of South Africa	Port Elizabeth	South Africa	Open	815	Ford PTE engine Zetec ROCAM	
Ford Motor Company of Southern Africa, Ltd.	Silverton	South Africa	Open	3,762	Ford Bantam Ford Fiesta Ford Tracer Ford Ikon Ford Ranger Mazda SOHO Mazda Etude Mazda Rustler Volvo S40 Volvo V40 Mitsubishi Canter Land Rover Jaguar	
Ford Motor Company Philippines	Santa Rosa, Laguna	Philippines	Open	719	Lynx Ford Tierra Ford Focus Mazda 323 Ford Escape Mazda Tribute	
Ford Motor Company ZAO	St. Petersburg	Russia	Open	1,571	Ford Focus	
Ford Otosan Assembly	Kocaeli	Turkey			Ford Transit Ford Transit Connect	Transit Connect starts shipping to US in Fall of 2009
Ford Otosan Engine	Eskisehir	Turkey	Open	1,676	Ford MT75 transmission for Transit Ford Puma engine< Ford Cargo truck Ford Rear Axle for Transit	
Geelong Aluminum Casting	Norlane, Victoria	Australia			engine parts	
Geelong Chassis	Norlane, Victoria	Australia			parts	
Geelong Engine	Norlane, Victoria	Australia	Open	644	I6 engines	
Geelong Iron Casting	Norlane, Victoria	Australia			I6 engines	
Geelong Stamping	Norlane, Victoria	Australia	Open	1,152	Ford Falcon body panels Ford Focus body panels (2011)	
Getrag Ford Transmission	Liverpool	England	Open	731	MT82 Transmission,	

						IB5 transaxle, MT75 Transmission, PTO Transmissions	
B (EU)	Genk Body & Assembly	Genk	Belgium	Open	4,600	Ford Mondeo Ford S-MAX Ford Galaxy	
	Hai Duong Assembly, Ford Vietnam, Ltd.	Hai Duong	Vietnam			Ford Laser Ford Transit Ford Ranger Ford Escape Ford Mondeo Ford Focus Ford Everest	
	Halewood Transmission	Halewood	England			Ford MT-75 transmission Ford IB5 transmission	
R (NA)	Hermosillo Stamping & Assembly	Hermosillo, Sonora	Mexico			Ford Fusion Mercury Milan Lincoln MKZ Ford Focus (01/00)	
	IMMSA	Monterrey, Nuevo Len	Mexico				
A (EU)	Ipiranga Assembly	Ipiranga	Brazil				
	Jiangling Motors Corp., Ltd.	Nanchang, Jianxi	China	Open	7,258	Ford Transit Isuzu	Partnership with Jiangling Motors Co., Ltd
K (NA)	Kansas City Assembly	Claycomo, Missouri	USA	Open	4,684	Ford F-150 Ford Escape Ford Contour Ford Escape Hybrid Ford Maverick (export) Mazda Tribute Mercury Mariner	
	Kechnec Transmission	Kechnec, Kosice	Slovakia			Ford MPS6 transmissions Ford SPS6 transmissions	Ford/Getrag dual clutch transmission "Powershift", (Getrag Ford Transmissions)
E (NA)	Kentucky Truck Assembly	Louisville, Kentucky	USA	Open	5,154	Ford Super Duty Ford Expedition Lincoln Navigator	
	Lima Engine	Lima, Ohio	USA	Open	730	Vulcan V6 Jaguar AJ35	

41

						Duratec 35	
	Livonia Transmission	Livonia, Michigan	USA	Open	1,849	AX4S 4R70W 6R	
U (NA)	Louisville Assembly Plant	Louisville, Kentucky	USA	Retooling	2,100		Will reopen in 2010 and build the Ford Kuga for European markets and the Ford Escape for North American markets. Lincoln Variant expected also.
	Metcon Casting	Santa Fe Province	Argentina			parts	
L (NA)	Michigan Assembly Plant	Wayne, Michigan	USA	Open		2012 Ford Focus and a Lincoln variant is expected also.	
S (NA)	New Model Programs Development Center	Allen Park, Michigan	USA				Commonly known as "Pilot Plant" Opened 1958
B (NA)	Oakville Assembly	Oakville, Ontario	Canada	Open	3,820	Lincoln MKX Ford Edge Ford Flex Lincoln MKT	Opened 1953
D (NA)	Ohio Assembly	Avon Lake, Ohio	USA	Open	1,821	Ford Econoline	Opened 1974, previously a Fruehauf truck trailer plant.
	Pacheco Stamping & Assembly	Buenos Aires	Argentina	Open	2,123	Ford F100 Ford Focus (until 2009) Ford Ranger Ford Focus II	
	Rawsonville Parts	Ypsilanti, Michigan	USA			Integrated Air/Fuel Modules Alternators Air Induction Systems Starters Fuel Pumps Carbon Canisters	Returned to Ford Motor Company from Visteon in 2005 after landmark deal with UAW
	Romeo Engine	Romeo, Michigan	USA	Open	1,160	Ford Intech engine Ford Triton engine	
K (EU)	Rheine Assembly	Rheine	Germany				
C (EU)	Saarlouis Body & Assembly	Saarlouis	Germany	Open	1,276	Ford Focus Ford Focus	Opened January 1970

						C-MAX	
B (EU)	Sao Bernardo Assembly	Sao Bernardo do Campo	Brazil			Ford Courier Ford Ka Ford F-Series	
	Sharonville Transmission	Sharonville, Ohio	USA	Open	1,478	Ford 4R70W transmission Ford 4R100 transmission Ford 5R110W transmission Ford 5R55S transmission Ford CD4E transmission Ford FN transmission	
	Southampton Body & Assembly	Southampton	England	Open		Ford Transit	
S (EU)	Setubal Assembly	Setubal	Portugal				
X (NA)	St. Thomas Assembly	Talbotville, Ontario	Canada	To close (2011)[1]	2,460	Ford Crown Victoria Lincoln Town Car Mercury Grand Marquis	Opened 1967
	Swedish Motor Assembly	Kuala Lumpur	Malaysia	Open	468	Volvo Cars	
	Taubate Chassis	Taubate, So Paulo	Brazil			Ford Fiesta components Ford Zetec engine components Ford Sigma engine	
	Tekfor Cologne GmbH	Cologne	Germany		352	Steel forgings	Joint Venture: 50% Ford; 50% Neumayer
	Thai-Swedish Assembly Co. Ltd.	Samutprakarn	Thailand				
P (NA)	Twin Cities Assembly Plant	St. Paul, Minnesota	USA	To close (2012)		Ford Ranger Mazda B-Series	Oldest vehicle plant, from 1924 Scheduled to be closed in 2012
P (EU)	Valencia Assembly	Valencia	Spain			Ford Explorer Ford Fiesta Ford Laser Ford Ranger Ford F-Series Mazda Allegro Mazda B-Series	

VIN Code (NA/EU)	Name	City/State	Country	Status	Employees	Recent Products	Comments
	Valencia Body & Assembly	Valencia	Spain			Ford Focus Ford Ka Ford Fiesta Mazda Mazda2	
	Valencia Engine #1	Valencia	Spain	Open	522	Ford Endura-E engine Ford HCS engine	
	Valencia Engine #2	Valencia	Spain			Zetec-SE engine	
	Van Dyke Transmission Plant	Sterling Heights, Michigan	USA	Open	1,260	Ford AX4N transmission Ford FN transmission Ford 6F transmission	
	Walton Hills Stamping	Walton Hills, Ohio	USA	Open	607	Body panels	
W (NA)	Wayne Stamping & Assembly	Wayne, Michigan	USA			Ford Focus (NA) Ford Focus (Int'l in 2011) Ford C-MAX (2011)	
	Windsor Engine	Windsor, Ontario	Canada	Open	1,850	Ford Modular engine 4.6 and 5.4 Ford Triton engine V10	
	Woodhaven Forging	Woodhaven, Michigan	USA			Ford Modular engine 5.4 parts Ford Triton engine V10 parts	
	Woodhaven Stamping	Woodhaven, Michigan	USA	Open	1,359	Body panels	

Former Production Facilities

VIN Code (NA/EU)	Name	City/State	Country	Status	Employees	Recent Products	Comments
A (NA)	Atlanta Assembly	Hapeville, Georgia	USA	Closed (2006)		Ford Taurus, Mercury Sable	
	Vintage Atlanta Plant	Atlanta, Georgia	USA	Replaced (1942)		Model Ts, Model As and V-8s	Southeast USA headquarters and assembly operations from 1915 to 1942
G (EU)	Barcelona Assembly	Barcelona	Spain	Lost (1959)			

	Batavia Transmission	Batavia, Ohio	USA	Closed (2008)	848	Ford CD4E transmission Ford U204 transmission	
	Bordeaux Automatic Transmission	Blanquefort	France	Sold		Ford C3 transmission	Sold to HZ Holding France SAS
C (NA)	Chester Assembly	Chester, Pennsylvania	USA	Closed (1961)			1927-1961, Demolished 2002
	Cleveland Aluminum Casting Plant	Brook Park, Ohio	USA	Closed (2003)			Aluminum engine blocks
E (EU)	Cork Assembly	Cork	Ireland	Closed (1985)		Tractor and car assembly	1917-1985
M (NA)	Cuautitlán Engine	Cuautitln Izcalli	Mexico	Closed			
M (NA)	Cuautitln Tool and die	Cuautitln Izcalli	Mexico	Closed			
A (EU)	Dagenham Assembly	Dagenham	England	Closed (2002)			Former products included: Ford Anglia, Prefect, Popular, Squire, Consul, Zephyr/Zodiac,Classic, Cortina, Capri, Granada, Fiesta, Sierra
E (NA)	Edgewater Assembly	Edgewater, New Jersey	USA	Closed (1955)			1929-1955 Replaced with the Mahwah Assembly Plant
T (NA)	Edison Assembly	Edison, New Jersey	USA	Closed (2004)		Ford Ranger Ford Mustang Ford Pinto	1948-2004 Demolished 2005 Also known as Metuchen Assembly
	Essex Aluminum	Windsor, Ontario	Canada	Sold (2009)	940	4.6L, 5.4L V8 & 6.8L V10 cylinder heads	Sold to Nemak; scheduled to close 1st quarter 2009
	Gaydon Assembly	Gaydon, Warwickshire	England	Sold		Aston Martin DB9 Aston Martin V8 Vantage	Sold to Aston Martin
	Green Island Plant	Green Island, NY	USA	Closed (1989)	close to 1000	Radiators, springs	Open 1922-1989. Demolished 2004
	Heimdalsgade Assembly	Copenhagen	Denmark	Closed (1924)		Ford Touring	1919-1924. Was replaced by, at the time, Europe's most modern Ford-plant, "Sydhavnen Assembly".
KC	Kansas City Assembly	Kansas City, MO	USA	Closed (1957)	3,200	Ford F Series	1913-1957. 12th Street & Winchester. First

	(Winchester)						Ford plant built outside Detroit area. Replaced by Claycomo plant.
C (EU)	Langley Assembly	Langley, Slough	England	Closed (1997)			Closed 1997. Former products included: Ford Transit and A-Series vans; D-Series, Transcontinental and Cargo lorries; R-Series bus/coach chassis
	La Villa Assembly	La Villa	Mexico	Closed (1984)			
	Leamington Foundry	Leamington Spa	England	Closed (2007)	398	Castings including brake drums and discs	Opened in 1940. Closed 07-18-2007.
	Long Beach Assembly	Long Beach, California	USA	Closed (1959)			1920 - 1959, Demolished in 1996?
J (NA)	Los Angeles Assembly	Pico Rivera, California	USA	Closed (1980)			1957 - 1980, Status of structure in Pico Rivera-Sold to Northrop Aircraft Company in 1982 for B-2 Stealth Bomber development. Demolished 2001. Plant only operated one shift due to California Air Quality restrictions. First vehicles produced were Edsels and Mercurys. Later vehicles were Custom, Galaxie 500, LTD and Thunderbird. Thunderbird production ended after the 1979 model year. The last vehicle produced was the Panther platform LTD/Crown Victoria in January of 1980.
H (NA)	Lorain Assembly	Lorain, Ohio	USA	Closed (2005)		Ford Econoline	Operations transferred to Avon Lake.
	Manukau Alloy Wheel	Manukau, Auckland	New Zealand	Sold (2001)		wheels	Sold in 2001 to Argent Metals Technology
	Maumee Stamping	Maumee, Ohio	USA	Closed (2007)	413	body panels	Closed in 2007
E (NA)	Mahwah Assembly	Mahwah, NJ	USA	Closed (1980)		Last vehicles produced, Ford Fairmont Mercury Zephyr	1955 - 1980 Demolished

	Newport Pagnell Assembly	Newport Pagnell	England	Sold	Aston Martin V12 Vanquish	Aston Martin now sold
M (NA)	Northville Valve Plant	Northville, MI	USA	Closed (198x)	Engine valves	Closed in the 1980s.
N (NA)	Norfolk Assembly	Norfolk, Virginia	USA	Closed (2007)	Ford F-Series	
	Omaha Ford Motor Company Assembly Plant	Omaha, Nebraska	USA	Closed (1936)		
C (NA)	Ontario Truck	Oakville, Ontario	Canada	Closed (2004)	Ford F-Series Ford SVT Lightning	
	Ford Richmond Plant	Richmond, California	USA	Closed (1956)	Various, WWII tanks and armored vehicles	Opened in 1930 and closed 1956 - Renovated, now part of Rosie the Riveter National Historical Park
R (NA)	San Jose Assembly Plant	Milpitas, California	USA	Closed (1984)	Ford Mustang/Mustang Shelby/Mercury Capri	Opened in 1955 and closed 1984 - now Great Mall of the Bay Area
	Seaview Assembly Plant	Lower Hutt	New Zealand	Closed (1988)	Ford Zephyr Ford Zodiac Ford Anglia Ford Falcon Ford Escort Ford Cortina Ford Sierra	Opened 1936. Closed 1988
Z (NA)	St. Louis Assembly	Hazelwood, Missouri	USA	Closed (2006)	Ford Explorer Mercury Mountaineer Lincoln Aviator	
S (NA)	Somerville Assembly	Somerville, Massachusetts	USA	Closed (1958)	Built Edsel Corsairs & Citations July-October 1957, Built Fords November 1957-March 1958	1926-1958, Converted to Assembly Square Mall in 1980
	Sydhavnen Assembly	Copenhagen	Denmark	Closed (1966)		1924-1966. Tractor accessory production until 1969, when Ford sold the building. Building stood until 2006. 325.482 vehicles were built.
J (NA)	TH!NK Nordic AS	Aurskog	Norway	Sold (2003)	TH!NK City	Sold to Kamkorp Microelectronics as of February 1, 2003
	Volvo Nedcar	Born	Netherlands	Sold	Mitsubishi Colt Mitsubishi Space Star	no longer Volvo, now 100% Mitsubishi

List of Chrysler factories

From Wikipedia, the free encyclopedia

This list contains all current Chrysler factories in North America.

Country	Name	Location	Date Opened	Current Products
Canada	Brampton Assembly	Brampton, Ontario	1986	Chrysler 300 Dodge Challenger Dodge Charger
	Etobicoke Casting	Toronto, Ontario	1942	Aluminum Die Castings, Pistons
	Windsor Assembly	Windsor, Ontario	1928	Dodge Grand Caravan Chrysler Town & Country Volkswagen Routan
Mexico	Saltillo Engine	Ramos Arizpe, Coahuila	1981,2009	Chrysler Hemi engine Chrysler Pentastar engine
	Saltillo Truck Assembly	Saltillo, Coahuila	1995	Dodge Ram 2500 &3500
	Toluca Car Assembly	Toluca, State of Mexico	1978	Dodge Journey Fiat Freemont Fiat Nuova 500
United States	Belvidere Assembly	Belvidere, Illinois	1965	Dodge Caliber Jeep Compass Jeep Patriot
	Conner Avenue Assembly	Detroit, Michigan	1966	Dodge Viper Viper V10 engine
	Detroit Axle	Detroit, Michigan	1917	Axles and differentials
	Indiana Transmission	Kokomo, Indiana	1998	Transmissions
	Jefferson North Assembly	Detroit, Michigan	1991	Jeep Grand Cherokee Dodge Durango
	Kokomo Casting	Kokomo, Indiana	1965	Aluminum parts
	Kokomo Transmission	Kokomo, Indiana	1956	Transmissions
	Mack Avenue Engine Complex	Detroit, Michigan	1953	Chrysler PowerTech engine
	Global Engine Manufacturing Alliance	Dundee, Michigan	2002	World Engine Fiat FIRE engine
	Mount Elliott Tool and Die	Detroit, Michigan	1938	Tools and dies, checking fixtures, stamping fixtures
	Sterling Heights Assembly	Sterling Heights, Michigan	1953	Dodge Avenger Chrysler 200

Sterling Stamping	Sterling Heights, Michigan	1965	Metal stampings
Toledo Machining	Perrysburg, Ohio	1967	Steering columns and torque converters
Toledo North Assembly	Toledo, Ohio	1997	Jeep Liberty Dodge Nitro
Toledo Supplier Park	Toledo, Ohio	1942	Jeep Wrangler
Trenton Engine	Trenton, Michigan	1952	Chrysler 3.8 engine Chrysler Pentastar engine
Warren Stamping	Warren, Michigan	1968	Metal stampings
Warren Truck Assembly	Warren, Michigan	1938	Dodge Ram Dodge Dakota

Factories to close under Chrysler bankruptcy	Location	Date Opened	Current Products
Kenosha Engine	Kenosha, Wisconsin	1917	Engines Chrysler LH engine
Twinsburg Stamping	Twinsburg, Ohio	1957	Metal stampings

Closed factories	Location	Date Opened	Date Closed	Products Produced
Newark Assembly	Newark, Delaware	1951	2008	Dodge Durango Chrysler Aspen
Pillette Road Truck Assembly	Windsor, Ontario	1975	2003	Dodge Ram Van Dodge Ram Wagon
Saint Louis Assembly North	Fenton, Missouri	1966	July 2009	Dodge Ram
Saint Louis Assembly South	Fenton, Missouri	1959	2008	"S" Body (minivans)
Los Angeles Assembly	City of Commerce Slauson @ Eastern	1920's	July 1971	"A" Body, "B" Body, "E" Body
Hamtramck, Michigan	"Dodge Main"	1914	1980	Dodge Brothers cars/trucks; "A" Body, "B" Body, "E" Body, "F" Body `Was the original Dodge Brothers facility.`

	Windsor Aluminum	Windsor, Ontario	Canada	Sold		Duratec V6 parts Jaguar AJ-V8 engine parts Ford Modular engine parts	no longer Ford; sold to Nemak
	Windsor Casting	Windsor, Ontario	Canada	Closed (2007)		engine parts	
Y (NA)	Wixom Assembly Plant	Wixom, Michigan	USA	Closed (2007)		Lincoln Continental Lincoln Town Car Lincoln LS Ford GT Ford Thunderbird	
H (NA)	Windsor/Walkerville Plant	Windsor, Ontario	Canada	Closed (1953)		Ford Modular Model T	opened 1904 and closed 1953
	Ypsilanti Plant	Ypsilanti, Michigan	USA	Sold		Starters Starter Assemblies Alternators C.O.P.	Originally owned by Ford Motor Company it then became a Visteon Plant later turned into an ACH Plant in 2006. It is said that Henry Ford used to walk this factory when he acquired it in 1932. The Ypsilanti Plant was Closed in December 2008. The Local UAW was local 849. Visteon
UK	Sydney Assemby Plant	Homebush, Sydney	Australia	Closed 1994		Ford Escort MK1 Capri MK1 Ford Laser Ford Telstar	Opened 1936, Closed September 1994

Some of the Automotive Jobs Lost in West Tennessee are on the Following Pages

AUTOMOTIVE FABRIC SPEICALTIES, INC.
620 Blanton Drive
Adamsville, TN.
Automobile and truck seat covers
1977   employed   180

HARMON AUTOMOTIVE, INC.
Division of Harvard Industries, Inc.
127 Tate Road
Bolivar, TN.
Diecasting, automobile and boat accessories
1963   employed   922

AMERICAN AIR FILTER COMPANY
2000 Tamm Street
Brownsville, TN.
Industrial heating, cooling air pollution and
Dust control equipment
1965   employed   300

IMC MAGNETICS CORPORATION
TENNESSEE DIVISION
Camden, TN.
Small electric motors
1980   employed   78

BEKAERT STEEL WIRE COPRORATION
Industrial Park
Dyersburg, TN.
Steel Cord
1986   employed   150

MURRAY CORPORATION
Sylvan Road
Dyersburg, TN.
Distribution automotive aftermarket center
1986   employed   70

COPELAND ELECTRIC COMPANY
957 Mullins Street
Humboldt, TN.
Engineering Electric Motors
1960   employed   321

BENDIX/ALLIED AFTERMARKET DIVISION
1094 Bendix Drive
Jackson, TN.
Packager and distributor of automotive parts
1973   employed   255

ANCHOR SWAN CORPORATION
1900 North Broad
Lexington, TN.
Industrial hoses   1977   employed   307

JOHSON CONTROLS
659 Natchez Trace
Lexington, TN.
Motor vehicle parts
1959   employed   559

A.O.SMITH AUTOMOTIVE COMPANY
MILAN AXLE PLANT DIVISION
Telecom Drive
Milan, TN.
Automotive assemblies frames, etc.
1978   employed   600

DOUGLAS & LOMASON COMPANY
Kefauver Drive
Milan, TN.
Automotive parts assembly
1976   employed   478

TOKEHEIM CORPORATION
Highway 77
Newbern, TN.
Assembly of gasoline dispensers
1980   employed   240

EMERSON ELECTRIC COMPANY
Paris, TN.
Bench Power Tools
1964   employed   429

HOLLEY CARBURETOR
Paris, TN.
Automotive carburetors
1974   employed   700

MIDLAND BRAKE CORPORATION
Paris, TN.
Heavy duty vehicle brake components
1965   employed   201

JAKEL MOTORS, INC.
Highway 57
Ramer, TN.
Small electric motors
1986   employed   100

ITT-AUTOMOTIVE
SWF AUTO-ELECTRIC
Highway 45 South
Selmer, TN.
Automobile electrical components
1969   employed   78

FAYETTE AUTOMOTIVE SPECIALTIES
Somerville, TN.
Car seat covers, convertible steering wheel
Covers and spare tire covers
1982   employed   121

PYROTEK INCORPORATED
Manufacturers Row
Trenton, TN.
Industrial gaskets and strainers
1978   employed   77

TECUMSEH PRODUCTS
1236 Manufacturers Row
Trenton, TN.
Hermetic Motors
1989   employed   250

GOODYEAR TIRE & RUBBER COMPANY
Union City, TN.
Tires   1967   employed   3100

This page left blank intentionally

GOODYEAR TIRE & RUBBER COMPANY
UNION CITY, TENNESSEE
JOBS LOST   3,100

A.O. SMITH AUTOMOTIVE
MILAN, TENNESSEE

JOBS LOST   **600**

Magnetek
Lexington, Tennessee   Employed 704

Allied After Market
Jackson, Tennessee   Employed 255

Johnson Controls
Lexington, Tennessee   Employed 559

Midland Brake
Paris, Tennessee   Employed 201

Emerson Electric

Paris, Tennessee   Employed 429

Holly Carburetor
Paris, Tennessee   Employed 500

Reitter & Schfenacker
Selmer, Tennessee   Employed 200

Harmon Automotive
Bolivar, Tennessee
Employed 922

Bolivar's Population

Before NAFTA 6,597   After NAFTA 5.802

CHAPTER FOUR

More Job Losses
For
West Tennessee

Brown Shoe Company

Brown Shoe Company was the anchor for many small communities where I lived and worked.

I remember growing up in the small town of Caruthersville, Missouri where the employees had what was considered at that time to be one of the best jobs available.

Brown Shoe employees were able to live the American dream. They could work their entire working lives with a company that was loyal to its employees. They could buy a nice home and raise their families in the town where they worked.

Brown Shoe facilities varied in size in this area from about 100 employees in Trenton, Tennessee, to almost 500 employees in Dyer, Tennessee.

Today Brown Shoe has suppliers all around the world. Tradekey.com numbers their suppliers as follows:

China 18 factories	U.S. 2 factories
Turkey 2 factories	India 2 factories
Russia 1 factory	Bulgaria 1 factory
Taiwan 1 factory	St. Lanka 1 factory

Today Brown Shoe Company manufactures a variety of shoes including:

Naturalizer
Famous Footwear
Dr. Scholls
Carlos
Naya
Buster Brown
Life Stride
Zodiac USA
Avia
Newados

Brown Shoe   Savannah, Tennessee

Brown Shoe   Lexington, Tennessee

Brown Shoe   Dyer, Tennessee

Brown Shoe   Trenton, Tennessee

Brown Shoe   Caruthersville, Missouri

Brown Shoe   Paragould, Arkansas

TUPPERWARE

Tupperware opened this factory in 1969 and employed 800 families when I began making sales calls in 1990.

That number reflects 1/3 of the entire population of Halls, Tennessee.

JOBS LOST 800

WILSON SPORTING GOODS

Operations began in 1978 at its facility in Humboldt, Tennessee.

In 1992 Wilson produced 96 million golf balls which was 17% of all golf balls production in the world.

In addition they produced 2 million dozen personalized golf balls.

JOBS LOST 650

AMERICAN OLEAN TILE

They began operations in
Jackson, Tennessee
in 1963 .
Manufactured ceramic wall and floor tile.

LOST JOBS 600

HUBBLE LIGHTING

Hubble began manufacturing industrial and commercial

lighting products at the Martin, Tennessee facility in 1965.

The down-turn in the economy had a devastated effect on

the construction industry and suppliers like Hubble.

LOST JOBS 325

CONSOLIDATED ALUMINUM COMPANY

They began production of aluminum sheet roll and
aluminum foil at the Jackson, Tennessee
facility in 1949

JOBS LOST 335

TOKHEIM INDUSTIES

They opened their facility in 1973 in
Newbern, Tennessee
Thcy manufactured fuel dispensers.

JOBS LOST 240

FOAMEX PRODUCTS
MILAN, TENNESSEE

They began production of their foam
products in 1960.

JOBS LOST 300

NCR

Their facility in Humboldt, Tennessee
opened in 1970
Producing MICR products and paper

JOBS LOST 77

CHAPTER FIVE

BUSINESS LOCATIONS
FOR SALE,
VACANT OR BEYOND REPAIR

BINSWANGER
AVAILABLE
404-892-4100

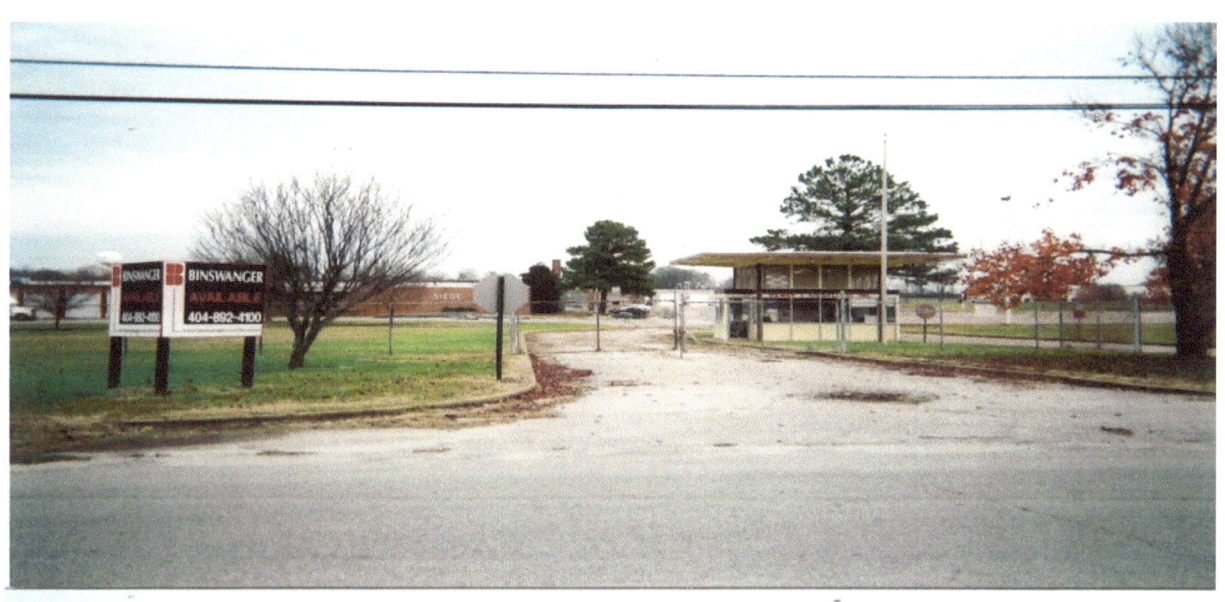

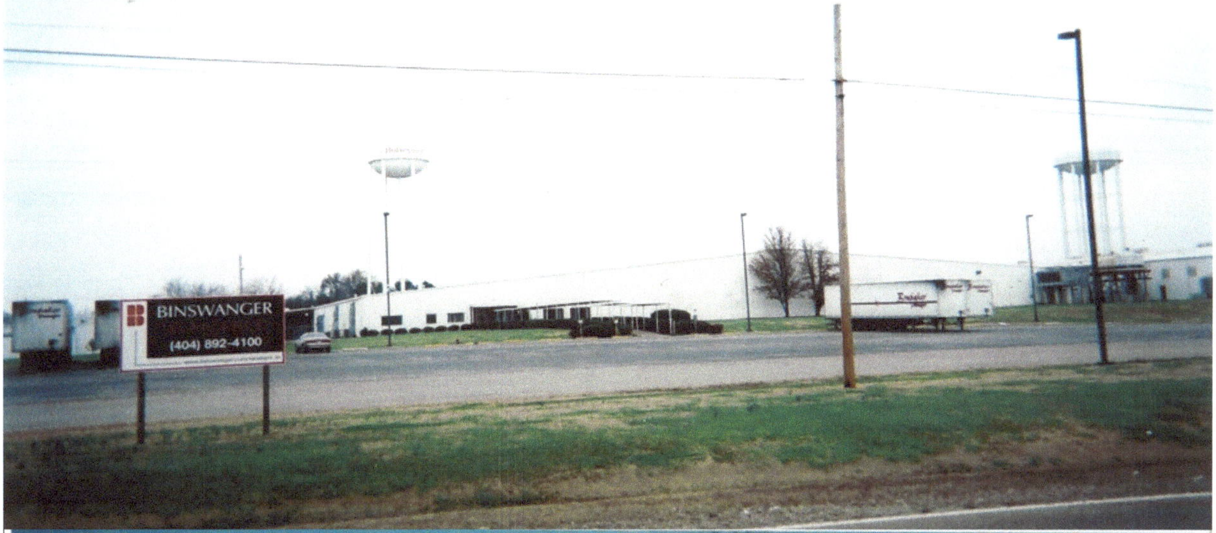
BINSWANGER
(404) 892-4100

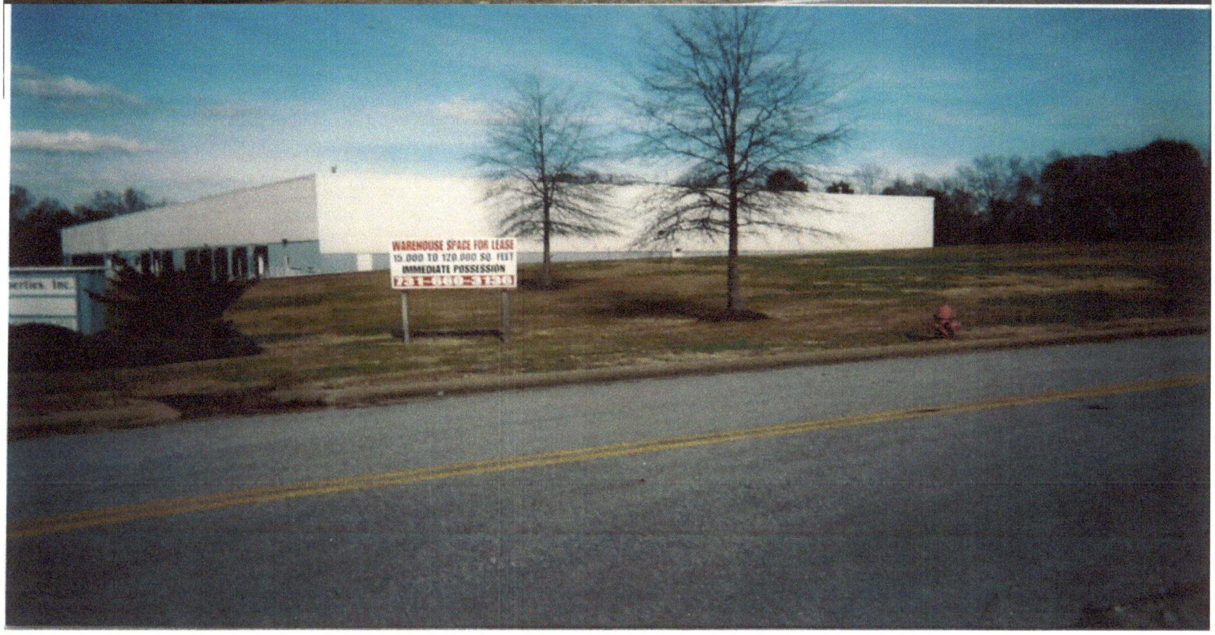
WAREHOUSE SPACE FOR LEASE
IMMEDIATE POSSESSION

Millions of square feet of
manufacturing and warehouse space are
available today in West Tennessee.

This page left blank intentionally

CHAPTER SIX

THE NAFTA SUPERHIGHWAY

NAFTA is a free trade and investment agreement that provides investors with a unique set of guarantees designed to stimulate foreign investment and the movement of factories within the hemisphere, especially from the United States to Canada and Mexico.

NAFTA tilted the economic playing field in favor of investors, and against workers and the environment, resulting in a hemispheric "**RACE TO THE BOTTOM**" in wages and environmental quality in the United States, Canada, and Mexico.

Economic Policy Institute

The NAFTA Super Highway

One of the trade agreements signed by Bill Clinton in 1994, The North American Free Trade Agreement (NAFTA), allowed for Mexican trucks to access United States highways into Texas, California, New Mexico, and Arizona by the end of calendar year 1995 and to all U.S. highways by the end of 2000.

U.S. trucks were to have the same access to Mexican highways. However, Bill Clinton and his administration did not allow the access due to concerns over hours-of-service and unsafe Mexican equipment. Instead, Mexican trucks were limited to commercial zones within twenty-five (25) miles of he border.

The restriction remained in place until July 2011 when Barack Obama and his administration signed a new agreement with Mexico. This agreement allows Mexican trucks to begin delivering Mexican exports to all points in the United States and loading Mexican imports back across our border.

Teamsters president, Jim Hoffa, said of the agreement, "We think its unsafe, unfair and wrong for America. This agreement caves in to business interests at the expense of the traveling public and American workers. Mexican trucks simply don't meet the same standards as U.S. trucks. Medical and physical standards for Mexican trucking firms are lower than for U.S. companies."

Despite opposition from the teamsters union, the independent truckers association and even members of congress, Mexican trucks may begin operations into the United States by the end of the Month (July 2011).

The Obama administration agreed to allow up to 900 Mexican trucks to begin operations within U.S. borders for the next three years.

These trucks will have on-board computer systems paid for with American tax dollars to ensure hours-of-service compliance. In addition, the computer system will track the Mexican trucks movements during the time they are operating in the U.S. The agreement allows for an additional 300 trucks per year until calendar year 2014.

Teamster president, Jim Hoffa continued, "This pilot program doesn't meet NAFTA's requirements that the Mexican government grant compatible authority to U.S. trucks. No trucking company or driver in his right mind would travel in Mexico under the State Department's current travel warnings."

Proponents of the agreement are using the same arguments as did Bill Clinton in 1993. Clinton promised the American people two million good paying jobs by 1998 and more markets for American goods. Instead, what we saw was exactly what Ross Perot predicted, "THE GIANT SUCKING SOUND OF JOBS LEAVING THE UNITED STATES."

Experience shows us that the American worker always suffers from this type of change. There will be thousands of driving and warehouse jobs lost in the United States when Mexican trucking companies begin rolling through this country.

Additionally, every American driver who buys gasoline or diesel fuel in order to operate his motor vehicle on U.S. highways, will be subsidizing Mexican trucking companies by paying road use taxes that build and maintain our roads.

The following pages show the proposed routes for the coming NAFTA Superhighway that will allow for the free flow of goods from Canada, through the U.S. and into Mexico and vice cersa.

Included are pictures of I-69 which begins in southern Texas and runs northward through Memphis, Tennessee to Ft. Wayne, Indiana.

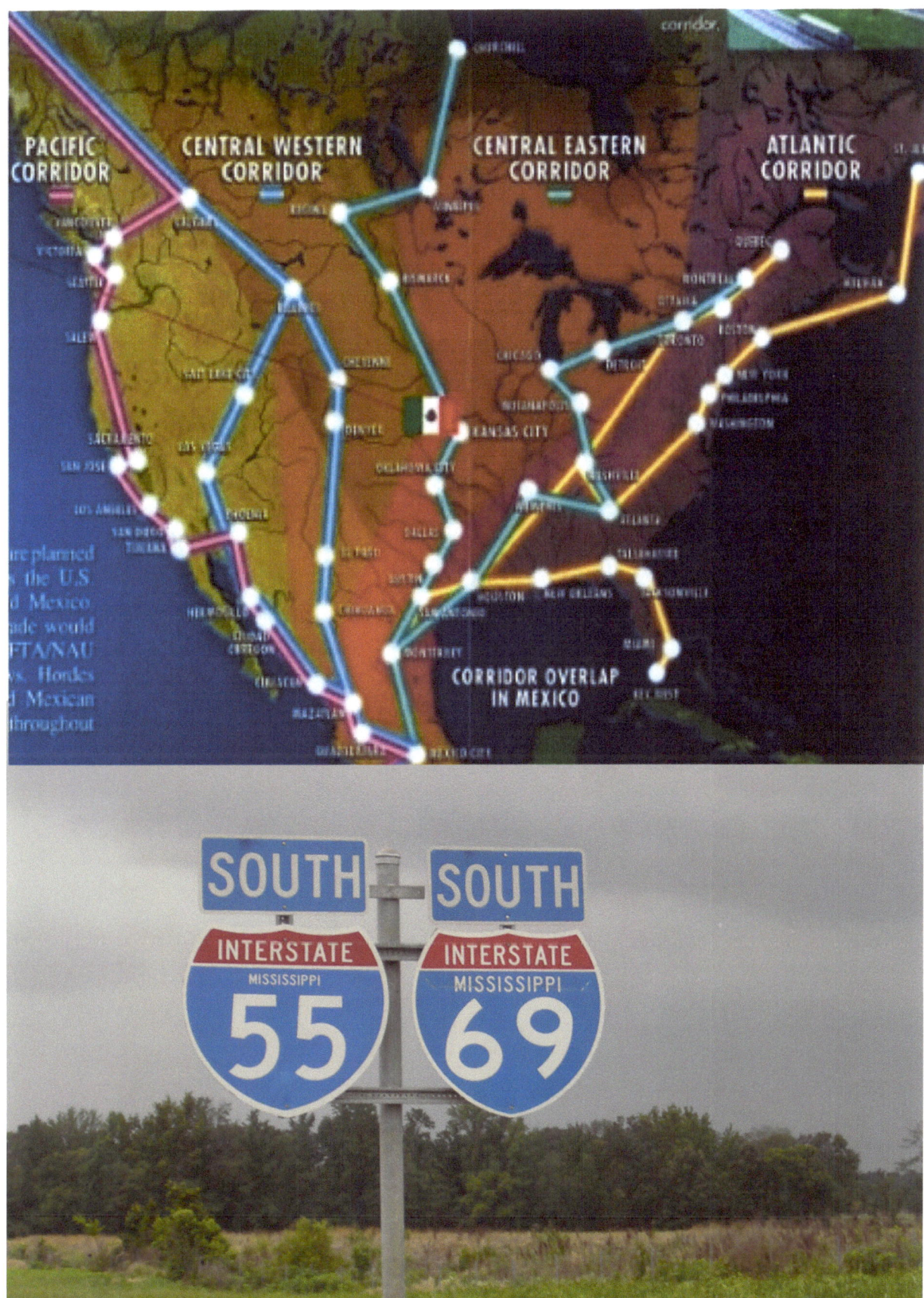

I-69 South from Memphis, Tennessee to Brownsville, Texas

This page left blank intentionally

Chapter
Seven

Ports
and
Containers

PORTS AND CONTAINERS

Bill Clinton considered the trade agreement he signed with the People's Republic of China the "centerpiece agreement of his presidency."

That, along with the other trade agreements Clinton signed, makes it virtually impossible to find manufactured products with the label that reads "Made in America." As a matter of fact the majority read "Made in China".

The job losses for manufactured goods were not limited to those working in the factories. The transportation industry took a major hit as well. By the year 2000 ninety percent of the less-than-truckload carriers in business when I started my career in 1978, had closed their doors.

Prior to the trade agreements, products manufactured in the United States were transported an average of four times before finally reaching the eventual user. After NAFTA , all the freight movement patterns changed forever and thousands of well paid Teamsters found themselves looking for new careers.

Less-than-truckload companies were hit hard because consumables now enter the United States as truckloads and move to warehouses and distribution centers around the country. Many of those warehouses and distribution centers have in-house carriers or are private carriers themselves.

Gone forever are so many of the trucking companies we grew up with. By the year 2000 we began seeing ugly rail boxes on chassis moving all around the country. The names on the container boxes were foreign to most of us and I still can't pronounce the names on some of them.. However, I am able to read "China Shipping" on the side of many of the chassis.

In west Tennessee we see truckload carriers moving containers to and from ports in Virginia, Louisiana, Mississippi and the Carolinas.

In addition, we have local companies moving containers into and out of the rail yards in Memphis, Tennessee. Railroads move containers to and from shipping ports around the country to keep the process moving.

The following pages show various trucking companies moving containers along I-40, a major artery across the country. Also included are the latest tonnage figures and the list of the world's busiest ports. Is it really surprising that six of the world's top ten ports for shipping containers are in China?

The following pages include pictures of those ports taken from the internet, along with pictures of containers moving along I-40 through west Tennessee. Remember, when you see containers, they represent one thing,

LOST AMERICAN JOBS.

Note: The pictures included in this work were taken from the internet and should not violate Homeland Security Regulations

Busiest Shipping Ports in the World

by BILL JAQUETTE *on* MARCH 1, 2011

At the each end of a major shipping lane is a major port, where cargo is loaded, unloaded, and even stored. Six of the world's 10 busiest ports are in China--measured in terms of cargo shipped in standard containers, or TEUs (20-foot equivalent units). Just two ports rival the amount of traffic flowing through Asia's busiest coastal cities--and neither are in the U.S.

1.

Singapore The world's busiest port handled more than 25.8 million TEUs last year.

2.

Shanghai, China China became the world's biggest exporter after surpassing Germany last year, and Shanghai was its busiest port with just over 25 million TEUs passing through its facilities.

119

3.

Hong Kong, China Last year Hong Kong handled almost 21 million containers.

4.

Shenzhen, China The second-busiest port processed over 18 million containers in 2009.

5.

Busan, South Korea South Korea's busiest port handled almost 12 million containers last year.

6.

Guangzhou, China The third port from a southern Chinese city in the Pearl River Delta, Guangzhou saw just over 11.1 million TEUs pass through its facilities last year.

7.

Dubai, UAE Last year 11.1 million containers passed through Dubai's port.

8.

Ningbo, China More than 10.5 million containers were handled by Ningbo Port, which competes with its much larger and nearby rival Shanghai International Port.

9.

Qingdao, China Last year Qingdao's container terminals processed 10.2 million TEUs.

10.

Rotterdam, Netherlands Europe's largest port reported that container throughput rose 16% to 2.6 million TEUs during the first quarter due largely to Asian trade. Almost 10 million containers.

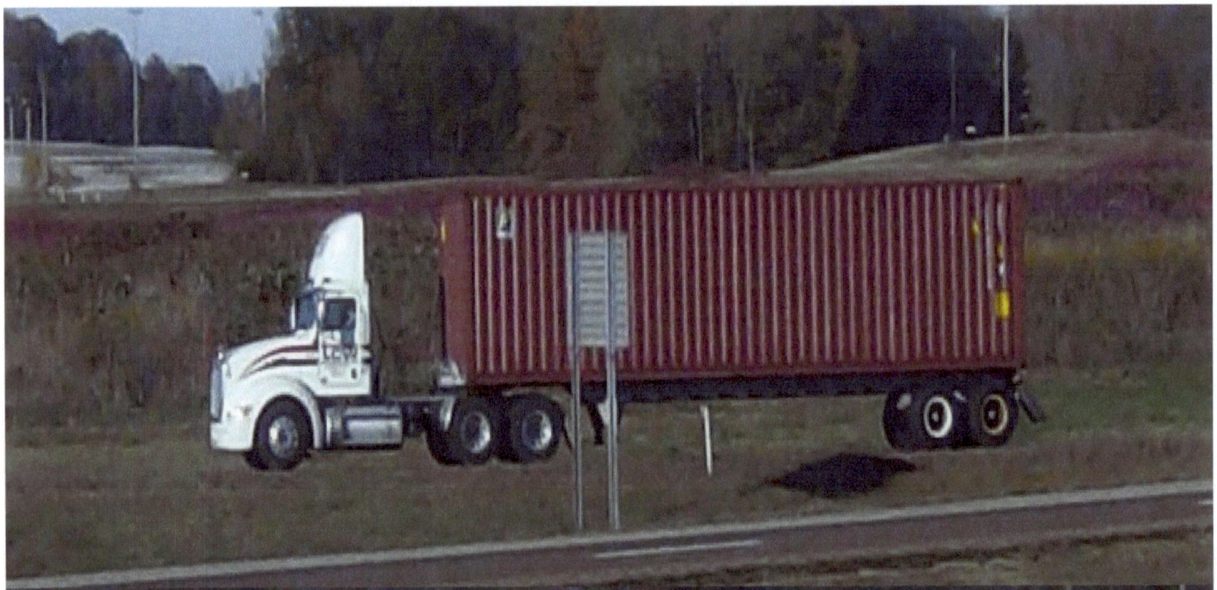

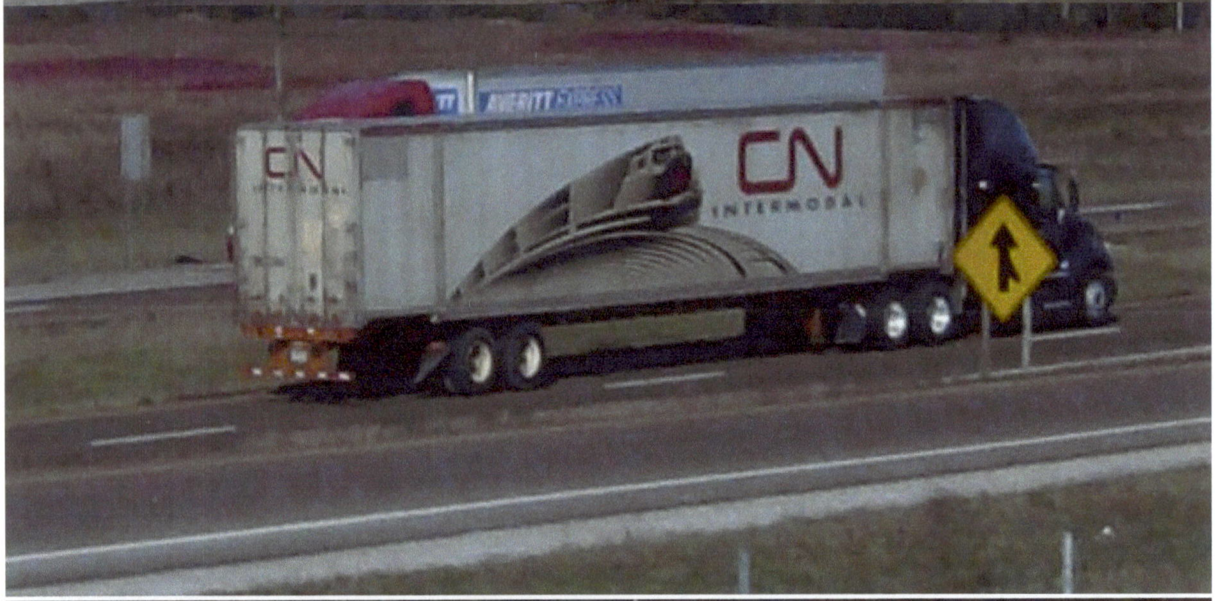
CN
CN
INTERMODAL

NO PARKING
MSC
NO PARKING

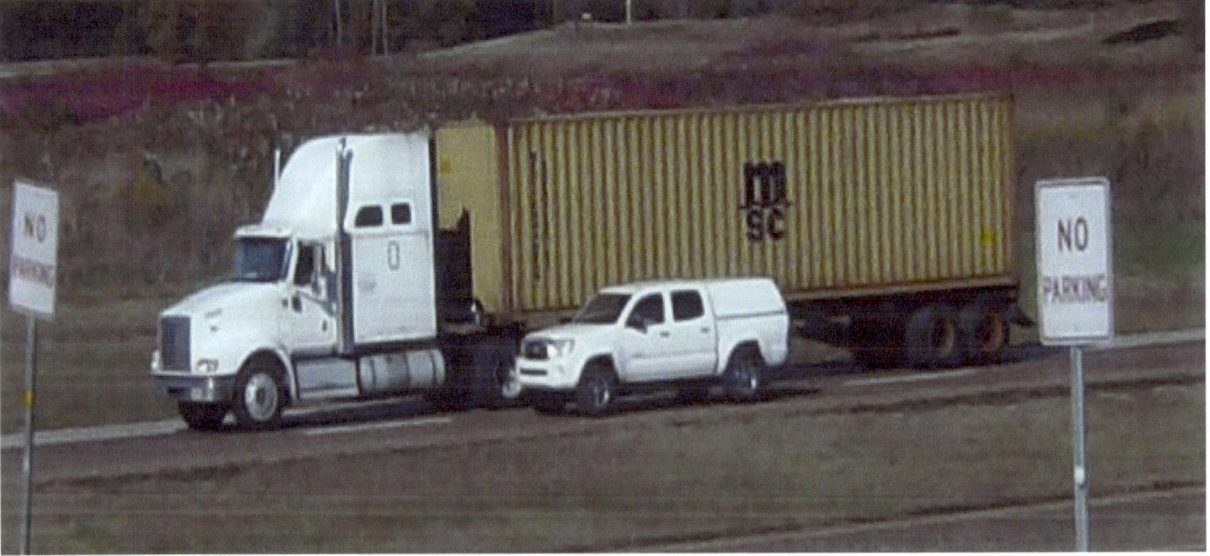

Chapter Eight

CONCLUSION

The national unemployment rate hit 9.7% last month which reflects a real number of 14.9 million people. Additionally, the underemployment rate is at 16.8%.

"The labor force grew by 73,000 people last month, which shows that some of those who'd dropped out of looking went back to the hunt. White House spokesman, Robert Gibbs, told reporters today that President Obama expects unemployment to hit 10% at some time this year."

----Planet Money by Laura Conaway

After almost twenty years of NAFTA , the results are in and we can evaluate what each of the "Faces of NAFTA" told the American people. Here is what Bill Clinton promised.

Right	Wrong	
_____	__X___	NAFTA means good paying American Jobs.
_____	__X___	NAFTA will create many more jobs than we lose.
_____	__X___	Mexicans will be able to support their families by staying home.
_____	__X___	There will be **LESS** illegal immigration
_____	__X___	Businesses will not be able to relocate solely because of very cheap wages.
_____	__X___	NAFTA is the debate over creating the jobs of the future.
100%	WRONG	

Here is what Vice-President Albert Gore, Jr. promised:

Right	Wrong	
_____	__X___	NAFTA means good paying American Jobs.
_____	__X___	NAFTA will create many more U.S . jobs than we lose.
_____	__X___	Mexicans will be able to support their families by staying home.
_____	__X___	There will be **LESS** illegal immigration
_____	__X___	Businesses will not be able to relocate solely because of very cheap wages.
_____	__X___	NAFTA is the debate over creating the jobs of the future.
100%	WRONG	

Here is what Ross Perot told the American people:

Right	Wrong	
_X_	_____	If you pass NAFTA you will hear "The Giant Sucking Sound" of jobs leaving this country.
_X_	_____	Do you guys ever do anything but propaganda?
_X_	_____	Would you even know the truth if you saw it, I don't believe you would.
_X_	_____	Save Your Job, Save our Country.
_X_	_____	NAFTA is not a trade agreement, but an investment agreement.
_X_	_____	The U.S. does not have enough GOOD jobs.
100%	Right	

..."Whatever else history may say about me when I'm gone, I hope it will record that I appealed to your best hopes, not your worst fears"   ... President Ronald Reagan—
Farewell Address to the Nation

Barack Obama ran for the office of President of the United States on the promise of "Change". Americans were really hoping for a new face and a reason to begin to believe in government again. Obama went to Washington with U.S. approval ratings for politicians running between fifteen and twenty percent. They had the lowest rating of any occupation in the country including used car salesmen and lawyers.

In January 2009 President "Hair On Fire" Obama couldn't wait to show the American people, and the world, that he was the next big government liberal and he was in charge by announcing, "There is no disagreement that we need action by our government, a recovery plan that will help to jumpstart the economy."

Obama and the Democrats who controlled the House of Representatives and the U.S. Senate pushed Obama's record spending bill through congress **WITHOUT DEBATE.** After all, Obama had already declared that there was no disagreement.

Actually, there was debate and plenty of it. A New York Times article on January 28, 2009 entitled "Economists slam Barack Obama's stimulus package by Alex Singleton stated:

"The line from Barack Obama and Joe Biden is that "ALL" economists agree with a stimulus package to expand government spending. So they won't be happy to see a full page advertisement in today's New York Times disagreeing, signed by 200 academic economists, including three Nobel prize-winners." According to Mr. Biden, "Every economist...from conservative to liberal, acknowledges that direct government spending on a direct program now is the best way to infuse economic growth and create jobs."

But the economists who signed the advert, funded by the Cato Institute in Washington D. C. say that, "we the undersigned do not believe that more government spending is a way to improve economic performance. More government spending by Hoover and Roosevelt did not pull the United States economy out of the Great Depression in the 1930's. More government spending did not solve Japan's 'lost decade' in the 1990's.

The Congressional Budget Office warned, "Obama stimulus **HARMFUL OVER LONGHAUL**." They said Obama's economic recovery package will actually hurt the economy more in the long run that if he were to do **NOTHING."** The CBO, the non-partisan Congressional Budget Office is the official scorekeeper for legislation, said the House and Senate Bills will help in the short term but will result in so much government debt that within a few years they would crowd out private investment, actually leading to a lower Gross Domestic Product over the next 10 years, than if government had done **NOTHING.**

Republicans and moderate Democrats have balked at the size of the bill and at some to the spending items included in it, arguing that they won't produce immediate jobs, which is the stated goal of the bill.

A Daily Pundit article on February 5, 2009 entitled "Porkulus Bill Stinks", was one of many to begin calling the bill what it was.

Washington-President Obama warned on Thursday that failure to act on his economic package could plunge the nation into a long-lasting recession that might prove irreversible, a fresh call to a recalcitrant congress to move quickly.

"This is just the rankest of hysterical justifications, the world will end if we don't spend $300 million to combat violence against women, $650 million for tv digital switch vouchers, $50 million for the National Endowment for the Arts, $1 billion for the census, $1 billion for climate research, $87 million for one icebreaking ship, $55 million for the Historic Preservation Fund, $159 million for honeybee farmers, and on and on and endlessly on".

"The American people won't buy it, and all of Obama's and the Democrats' hysterical demands for passage of this "Socialist Wet Dream" aren't going to make it smell any better".

An article by the Daily Caller on September 19,2011 entitled, "How Obama's stimulus bill became a comedy of errors,"

Remember, Obama promised the American people that if his stimulus package passed, unemployment would not go past 8%. In September 2011 Obama says he expects that figure to exceed 10% before the end of the year.

The Daily Caller article broke down the results of the stimulus:

The $825 billion extravaganza, touted as an emergency measure, targeted sectors of the economy with the lowest unemployment rates-government employees. (2.3 percent unemployed), in particular those in schooling and health care. (3.8 percent unemployed). By contrast, unemployment rates in manufacturing and construction were 8.3 percent and 15.2 percent respectively.

Obama's stimulus provided the least help to the states hardest-hit by the recession. Michigan had a 15.2 percent unemployment rate and the Obama stimulus created or saved only 400 jobs. Businesses in Nevada, which had the second highest unemployment rate, reported 159 jobs created or saved. And businesses in Rhode Island, which had the third highest unemployment rate, 12.8%, reported only six (6) jobs created.

Meager though these numbers were, in October 2009 Obama's top economist, Christian Romer, testified before Congress that the effects of the stimulus were leveling off.

Moreover, the government was slow about getting the money out the door, and many economists believe it didn't stimulate anything.

Six months after the stimulus bill became law, less than 20% of the money had been spent, and Obama was claiming it had funded about 30,000 jobs—not much compared with the approximately 10 million people who were unemployed.

The Associated Press reviewed some of the stimulus contracts and reported that the administration's claim of 30,000 jobs was exaggerated by about 5,000. White House sources said the administration was working to correct errors.

Then, according to The New York Times, Obama administration officials released new information purported to show that the stimulus had "saved or created" 640,239 jobs, of which 325,000—more than half—were held by members of teacher's unions.

In New York the number of teacher's jobs saved was inflated to include those jobs Mayor Bloomburg was negotiating a contract for during his re-election, so it would be hard to credit stimulus money with those jobs.

The Boston Globs reported that, "while Massachusetts recipients of federal stimulus money collectively reported 12,374 jobs saved or created, our review shows that number is wildly exaggerated."

Organizations that received stimulus money miscounted jobs, filed erroneous figures, or claim jobs for work not yet started.

On another occasion after the Obama Administration claimed to have created or saved 60,000 jobs, it acknowledged that the number was bogus—arising from "unrealistic data."

The General Services Administration reportedly spent $84 million developing the official Recovery.Com website that announced jobs saved or created in non-existent congressional districts, like Arizona's 15th (Arizona only has eight congressional districts).

North Dakota's 99th (the state has only ONE congressional district).

440 Non-Existent congressional districts reported jobs saved or created.

If we accept the original claims of a million jobs were " created or saved", the total amount of stimulus money spent was $160 billion, which would mean each job cost the TAX-PAYERS $160,000 each.

A Cato Institute economist, Alan Reynolds, estimates that each government job cost an estimated $646,000.

Six million dollars went to save three (6) jobs at Burson-Marsteller, a public relations firm headed by Hillary Clinton's former pollster, Mark Penn.

Another Obama payout went to people who "bundled" money for his presidential campaign. His administration granted loan guarantees to a start-up "GREEN" company called Solyndra to produce solar panels. Within two years of receiving more than $500 million in loans guaranteed by U.S. Taxpayers, the company filed bankruptcy.

On May 26, 2010 Obama touted Solyndra as "The Future of America". Today they are bankrupt and 1,100 more people are unemployed.

While on his latest vacation at Martha's Vineyard, Obama promised the American people a new jobs bill. In speeches around the country Obama said the words "pass my bill' more than 90 times. Ironically, during most of the speeches where he told people "if you love me, pass my bill", there was no bill. He had not produced anything for any member of congress to present in either house.

Finally Obama has presented his newest jobs proposal at a cost to American taxpayers of $450 Billion.

Fortunately the Republicans control the House of Representatives and Senate majority whip, Dick Durbin stated, "the Democrats don't have the votes in the Senate either." On Friday Durbin stated, "We, don't have the votes in the Senate to pass Obama's jobs bill. "

He added, "The oil-producing states senators don't like eliminating or reducing the subsidy for oil companies. And, there are some (Democratic) senators who are up for election who say I'm never gonna vote for a tax increase while I'm up for election, even on the wealthiest people. So, we're not gonna have 100% Democratic Senators."

As this was happening, the Obama energy department was doubling down on it's $500 million losses in green energy technology bys issuing U.S. taxpayer guaranteed loans to a company called Mojave Energy, the massive new energy project insane Bernadino, California.

The project is projecting 900 construction and permanent jobs. Let's see, Solyndra claimed to have produced 1,100 jobs for less than half of MoJave Energy's award before it went bankrupt.

News reports on Friday were stating that a brother-in-law of former speaker –of-the-house, Nancy Pelosi, was a player in this billion dollar award. Isn't this the type of dirty politics that presidential candidate Barack Obama promised to end when he became president????

In June 2011, President Obama traveled to Iowa to tout his latest "jobs bill", and asked Americans to have patience with the sluggish economy. During his speech Obama stated, "the Solution is not in Washington."

At this point most Americans agree with Obama. We KNOW that many of those who voted for the trade agreements that cost us our jobs, refuse to do what is necessary to either bring jobs back to this country or create new ones.

It has become obvious, at least to this author, that, in order to provide jobs for our children and grandchildren, we must first eliminate the job of the career politician.

Only when the politician really fears for his job, will American workers be secure in theirs.

The Obama Legacy

- **U.S. Population**   **312,336,984**
- **U.S. Income Taxpayers**   **112,219,481**
- **Official Unemployed**   **13,898,862**
- **Actual Unemployed**   **24,854,377**
- **Food Stamps**   **46,000,000**
- **Foreclosures**   **1,000,000**
- **Bankruptcies**   **1,600,000**

End Notes

1. Directory of West Tennessee Manufacturers 1988-1989
    West Tennessee Industrial Association-Jackson, TN.
2. West Tennessee Industrial Guide 2010
    West Tennessee Industrial Association-Jackson, TN.
3. NAFTA — Embracing Change Bill Clinton's Speech
    To the Nation. History.com
4. President Bill Clinton signs NAFTA into law.
    You tube @youtube.com
5. Barrack Obama and Hillary Clinton debate changing
    The NAFTA agreement, YouTub @youtube.com
6. Al Gore and Ross Perot debate NAFTA
    You tube @youtube.com
7. Ross Perot and the Giant Sucking Sound of Jobs leaving
    This country, you tube @youtube.com
8. The Ten fastest dying U.S. Industries,
    ABC News money segment April 5, 2011
9. U.S. Textile makers seeking tariffs against Chinese
    Imports, Thomas Russell, furniture today 07 25, 2011
10. Toyota Camry "Most American Car",
    Cars.com index for 2011
11. General Motors Parts Suppliers and Factories
    Wikipedia.org/Wiki/List-of-GM factories website.
12. Ford parts suppliers and factories
    Wikipedia.org
13. Chrysler parts suppliers and factories
    Wikipedia.org
14. NAFTA "race to the bottom"
    Economic policy institute.
15. Pictures provided by Wikipedia.org.
16. Pictures provided by Starpluse.com
17. Pictures provided by Billjaquette.net
18. Obama's fake job scheme
    Heritage foundation, webmaila.juno.com
19. Pictures provided by logisticsmgmt.com/images
20. Pictures provided by futurity.org
21. Pictures provided by media-2.web.britannica.com
22. Pictures provided by davis commercial investments.com
23. Pictures provided by 2.bp.blogspot.com
24. Solyndra shows the folly of 09 stimulus bill
    dailyworld@wwwdailyworld.com/article 2
25. How Obama's last stimulus bill became a comedy of errors
    Jim Powell the Daily Caller 09 19 2011@ dailycaller.com
26. Economist slam Obama stimulus package
    Alex Singleton politics 01 28 2009@bolgs.telegraph.co.uk/news
27. CBO: Obama stimulus harmful over longhaul
    Steven Dinan, the Washington Times 02 04 2009@www.washingtontimes.com/news
28. Finding the pork in Obama's stimulus bill
    Matthew Bandyk, U.S. News and World Report@ money.usnews.com/money/business-economy

How have the closings affected you, your family, friends and co-workers in the West Tennessee area?

For those of you outside the West Tennessee area, we would love to hear from you and get your information about the closings of factories, companies and businesses where you live. If you would like to submit your information…

Contact Us At:
jobswherearethey@juno.com
Copyright© 2011 by Neal Morgan

First Edition

Jobs? Where Are They?

Cover, Text Design, Typography by Carol Pillow